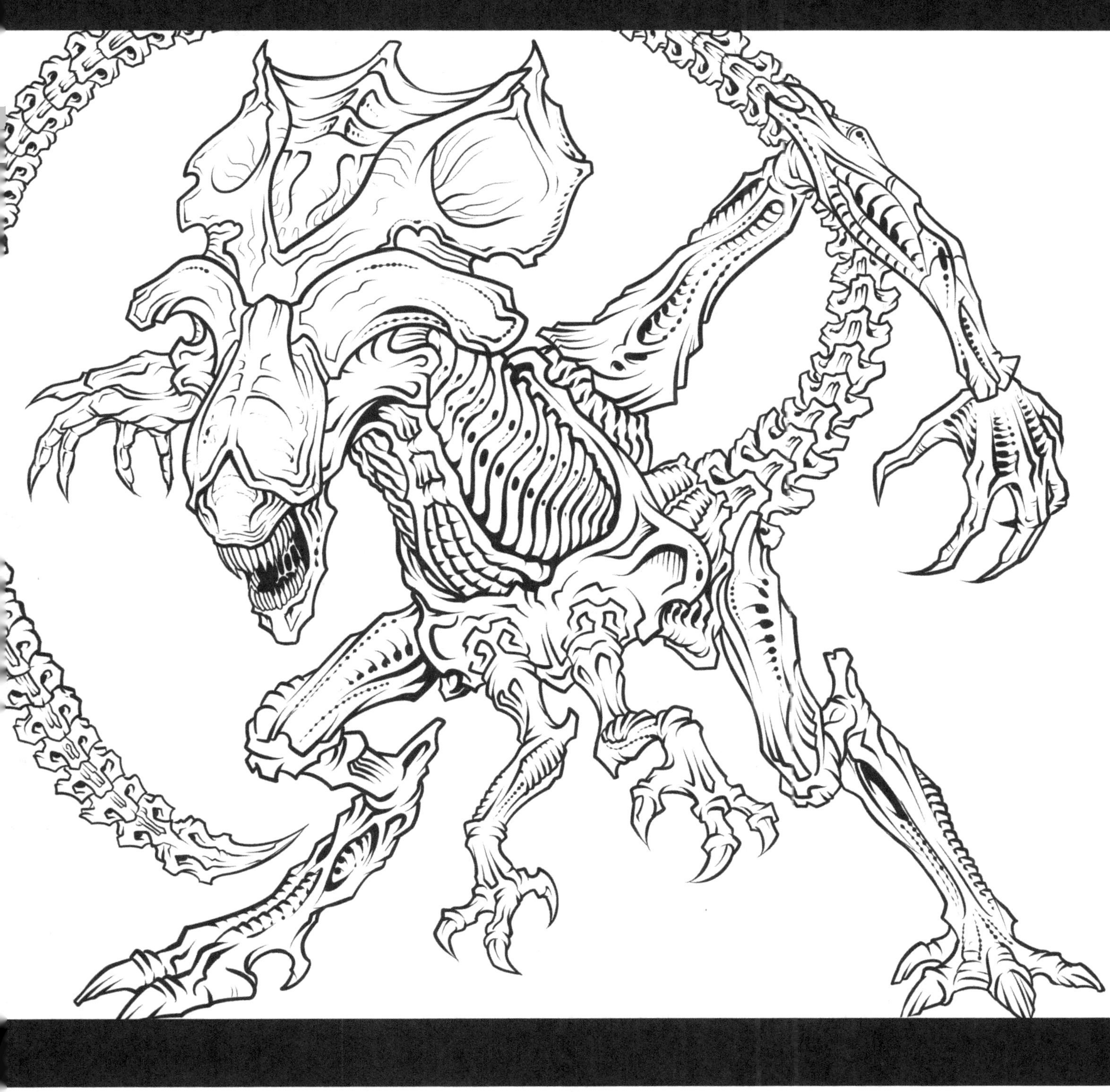

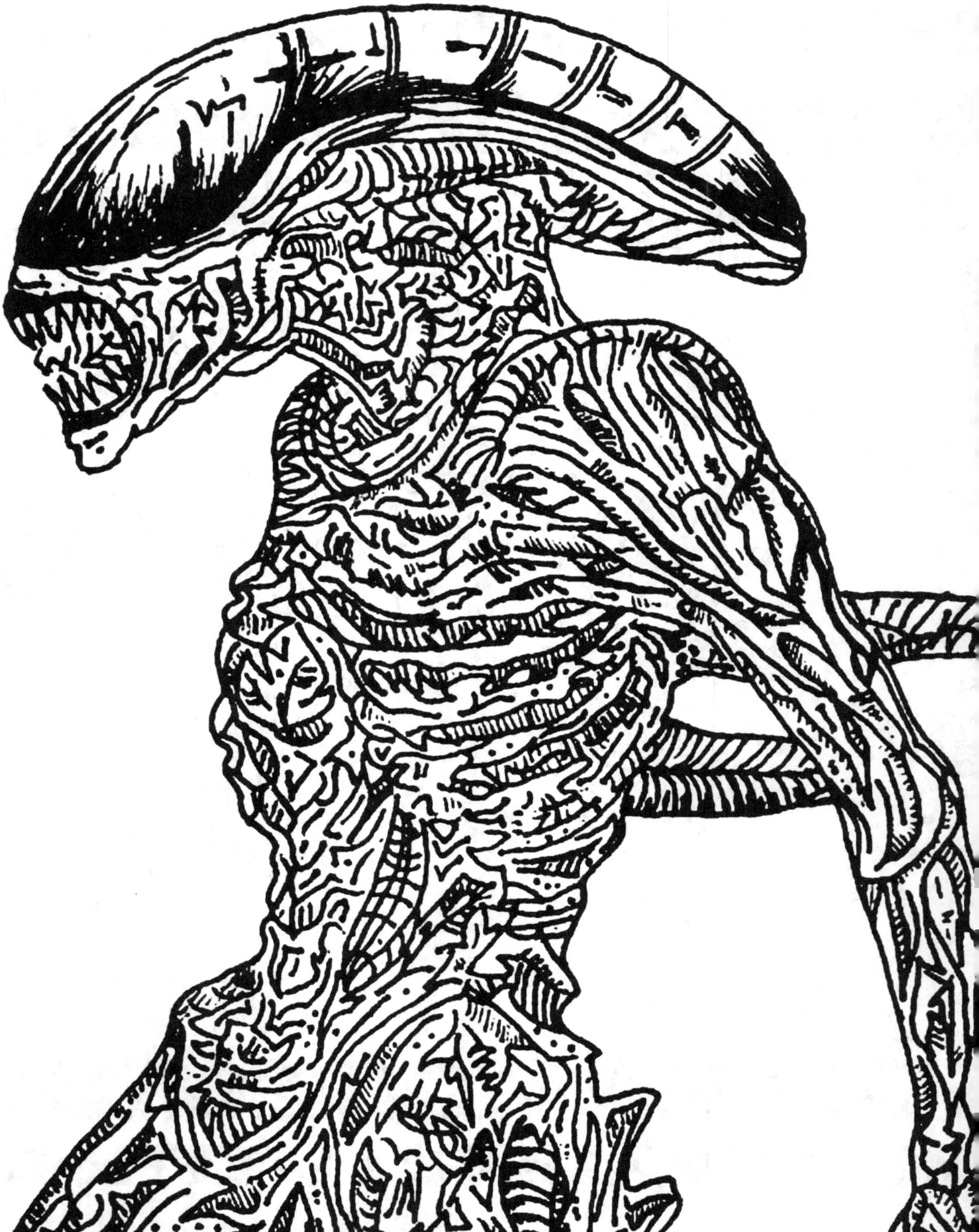

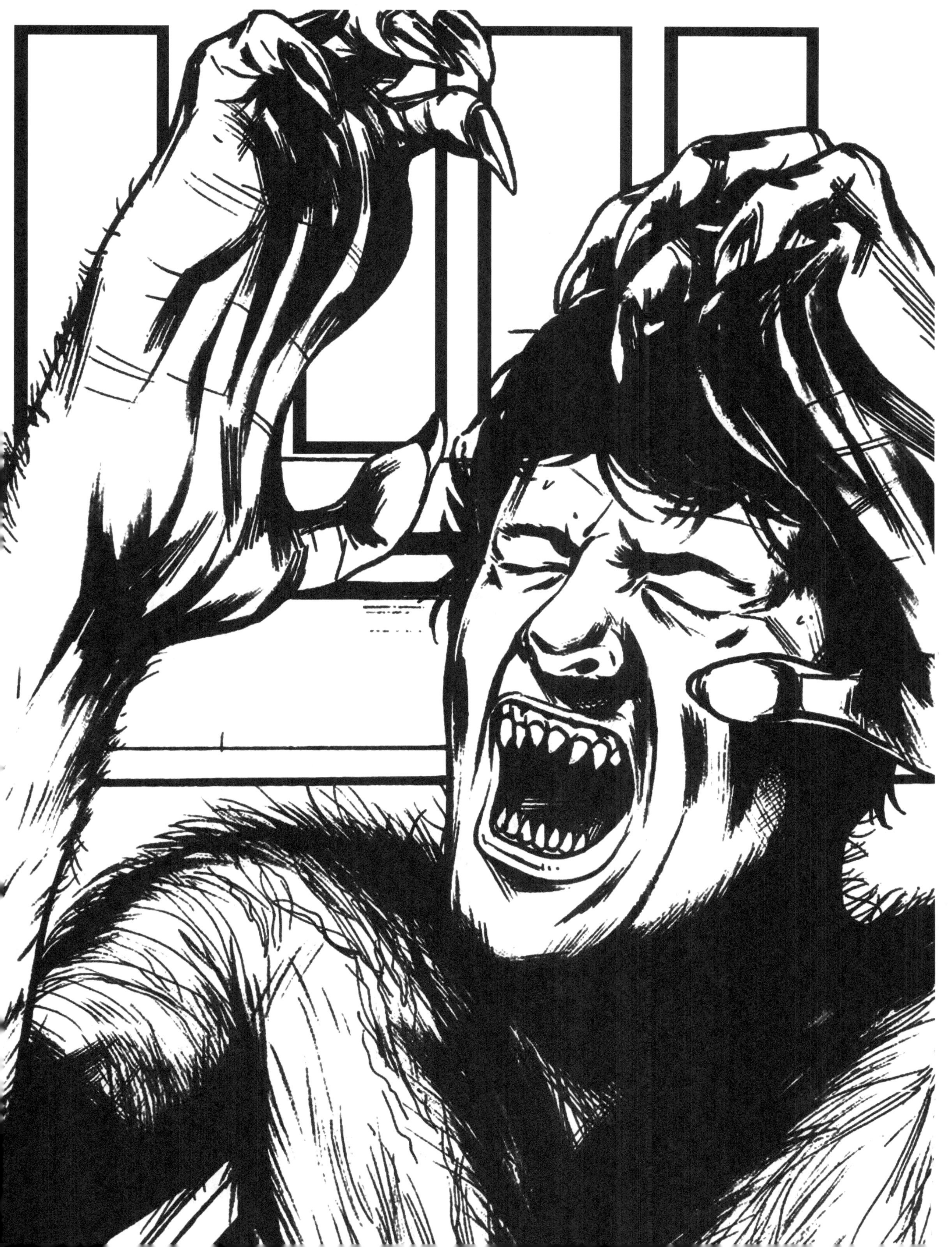

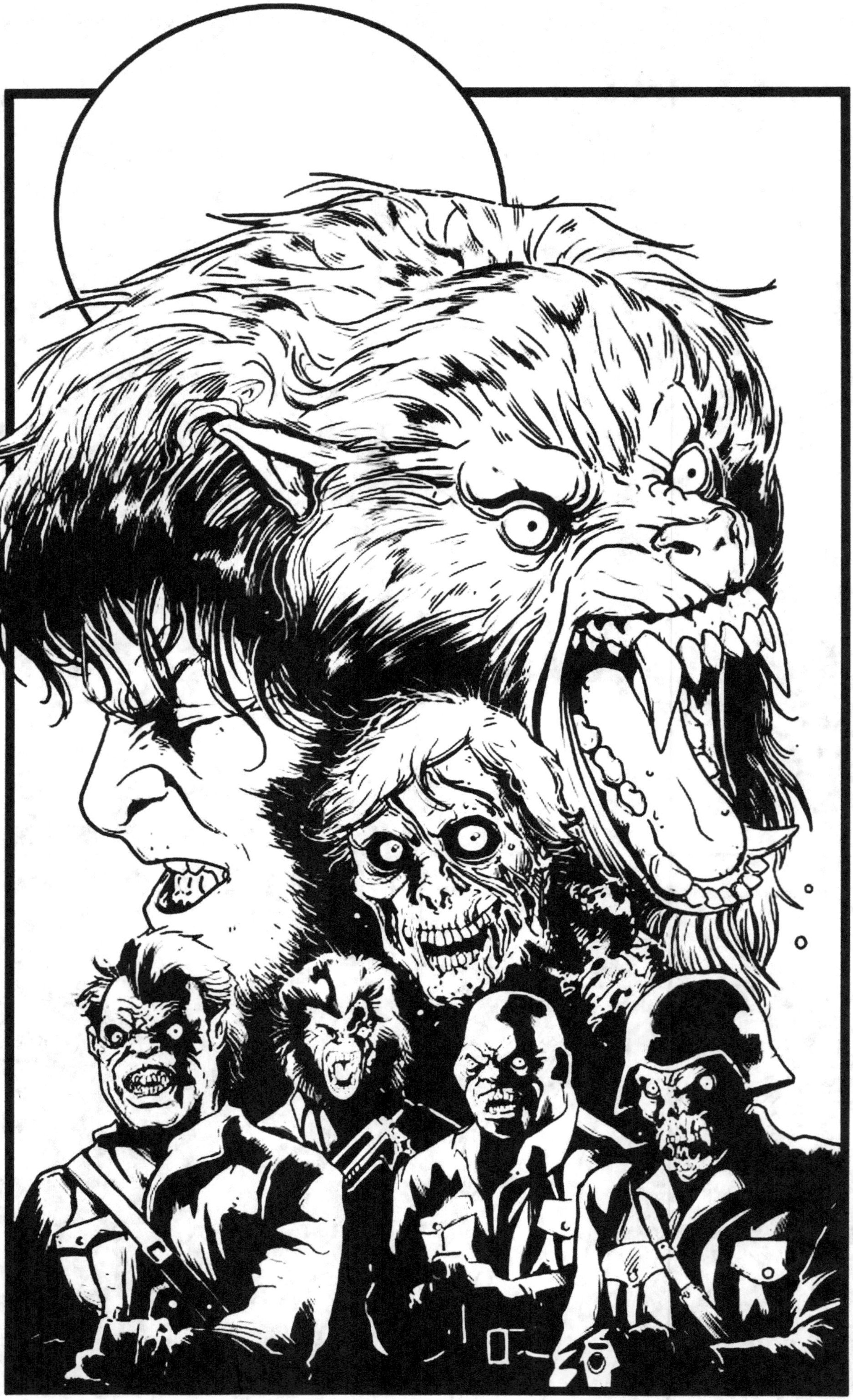

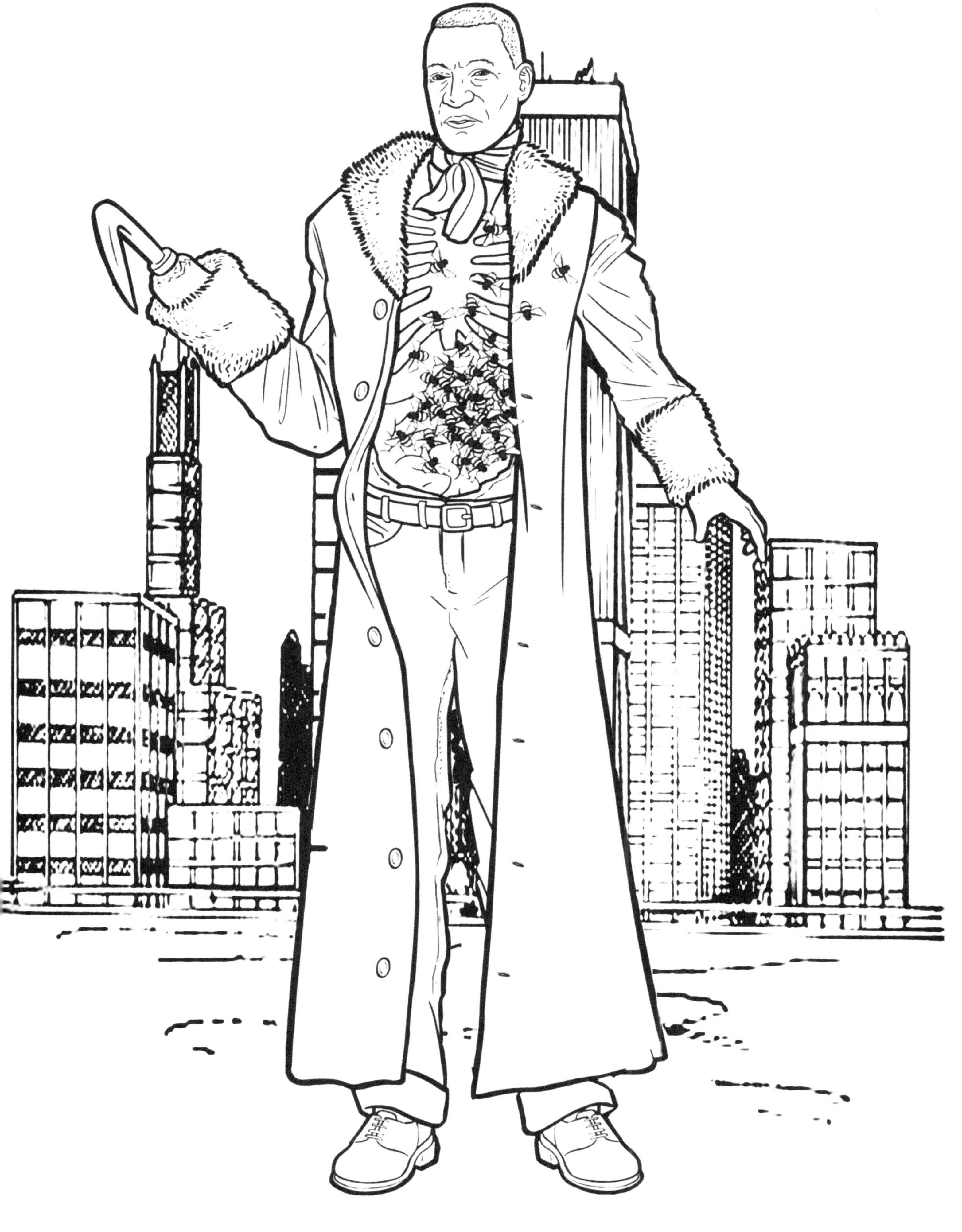

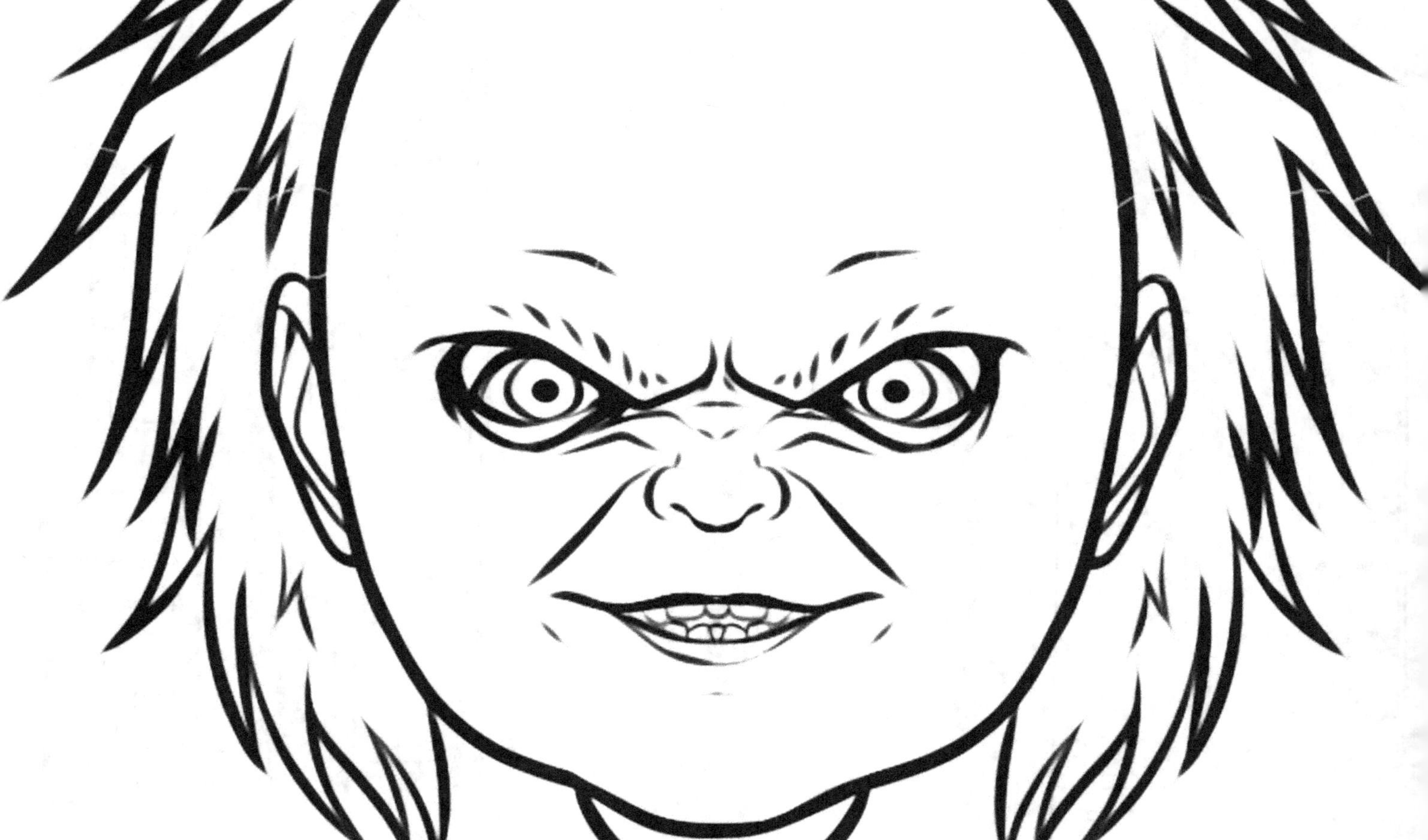

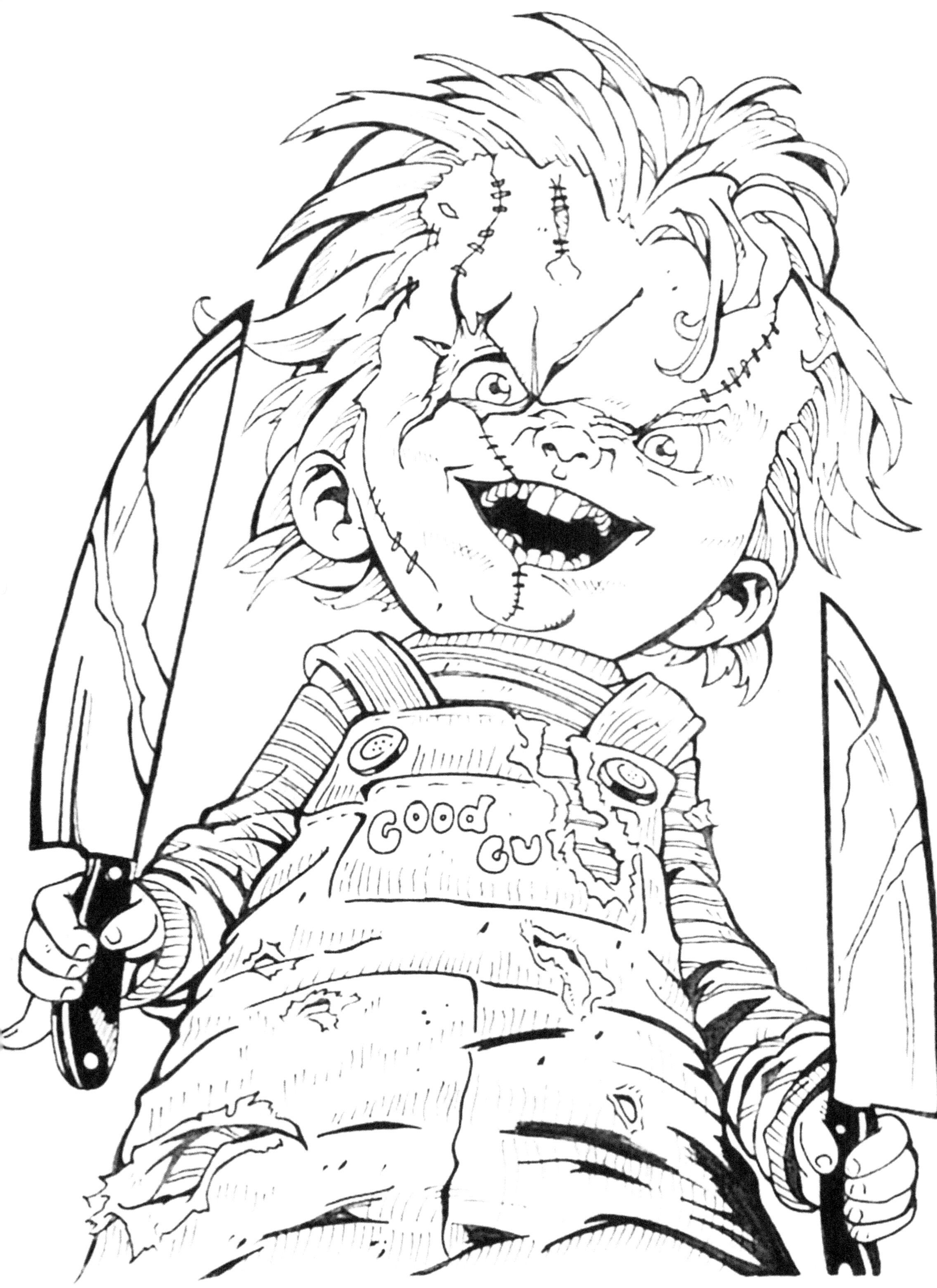
Good
Gu

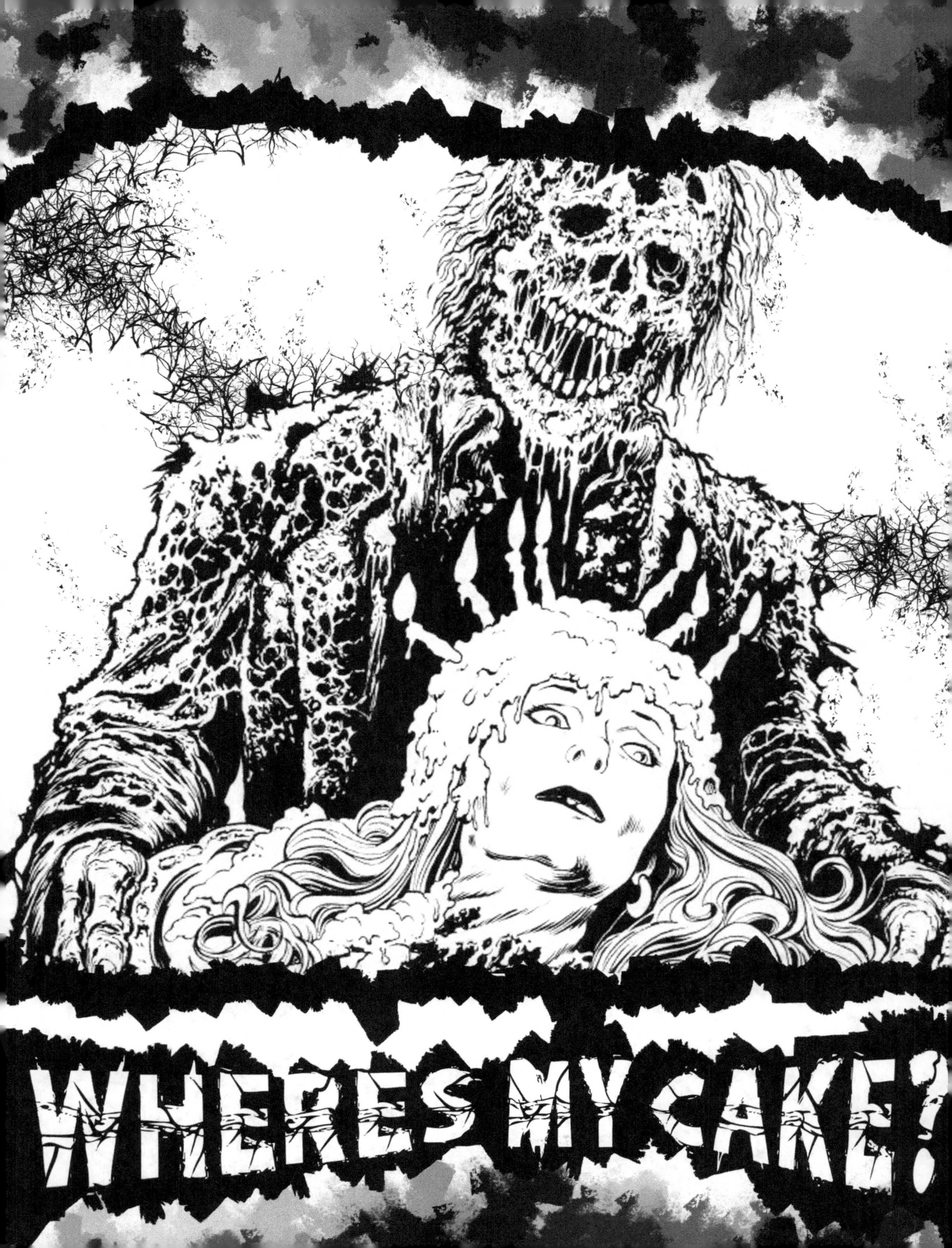
WHERES MY CAKE?

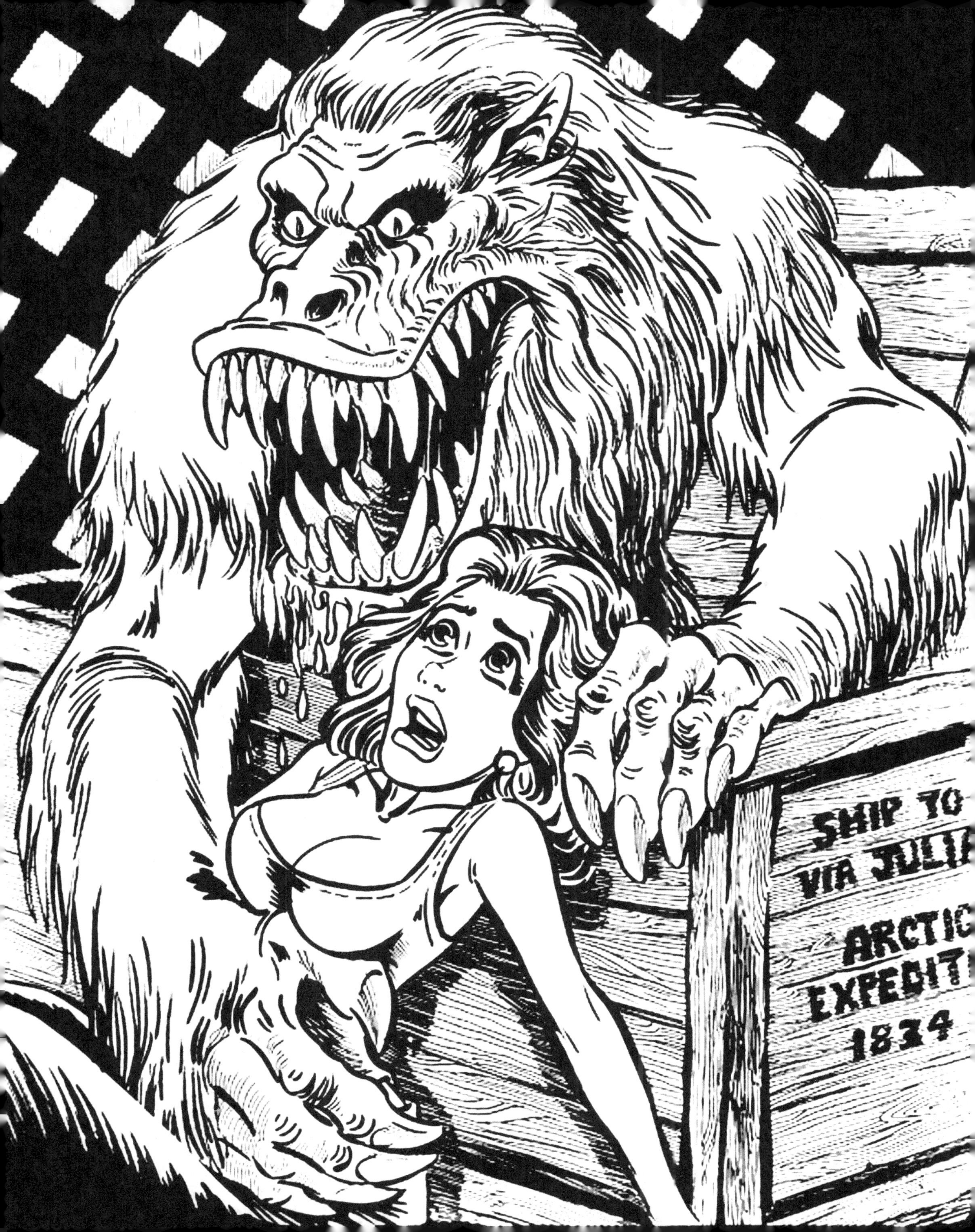
SHIP TO
VIA JULI
ARCTIC
EXPEDIT
1834

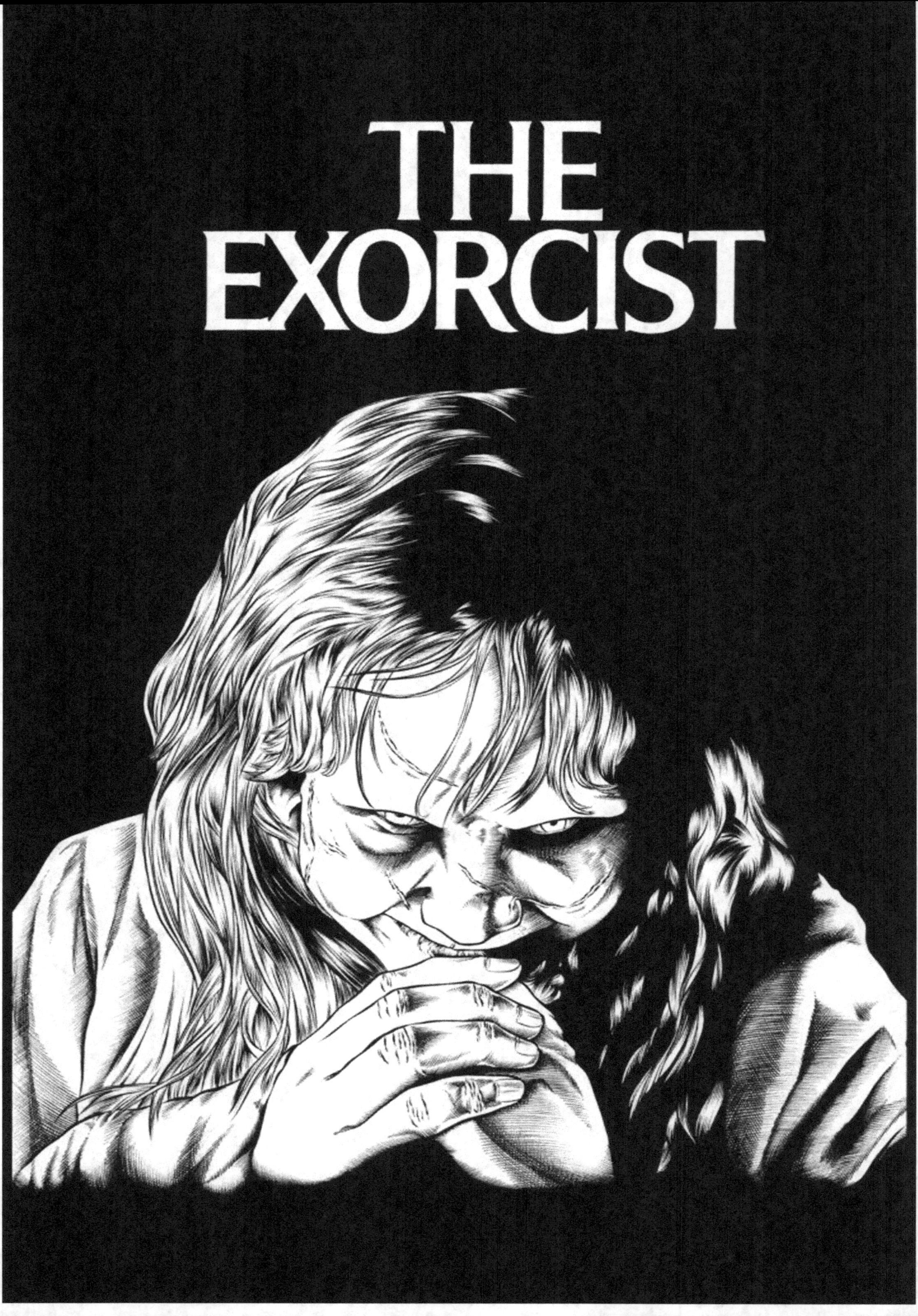
THE
EXORCIST

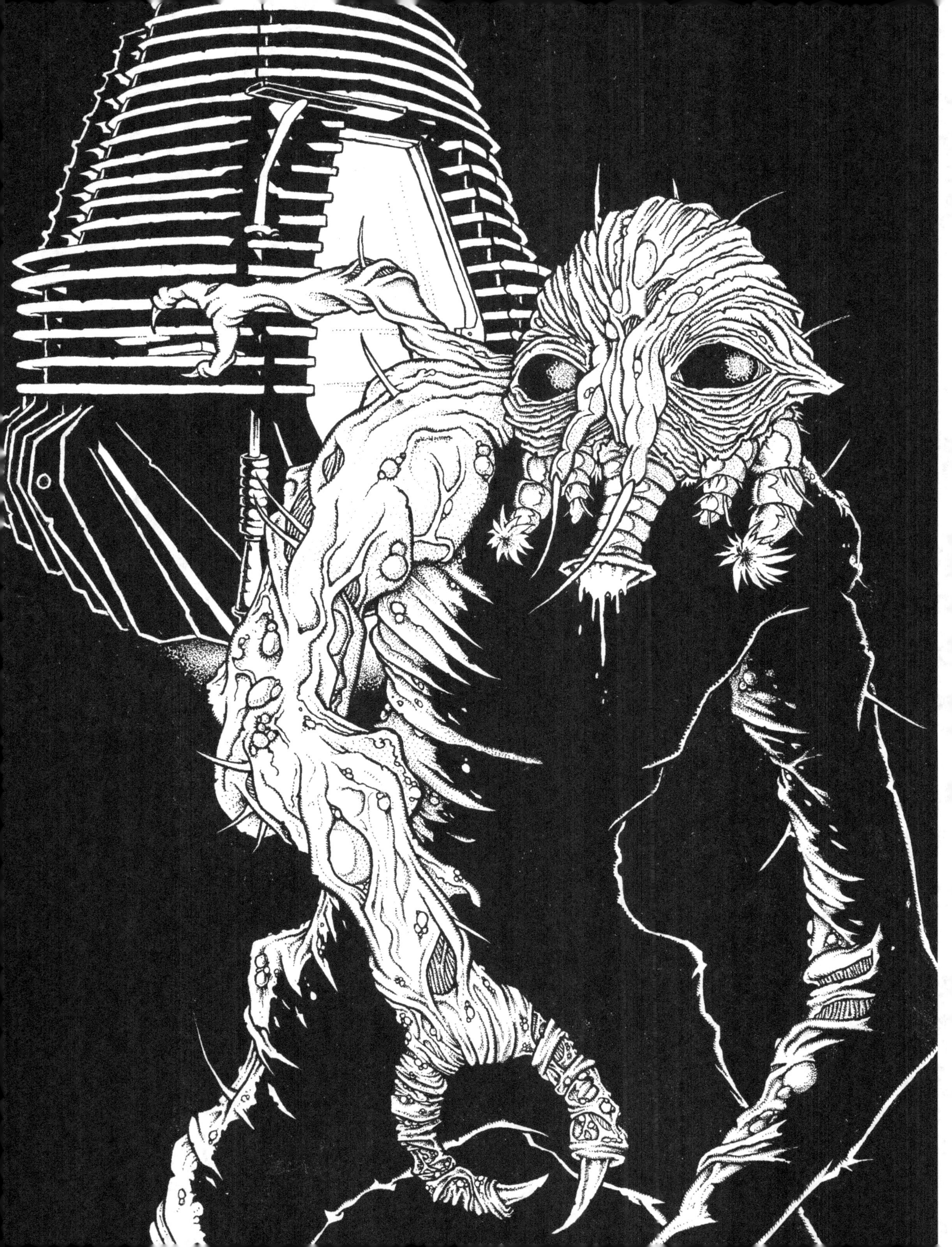

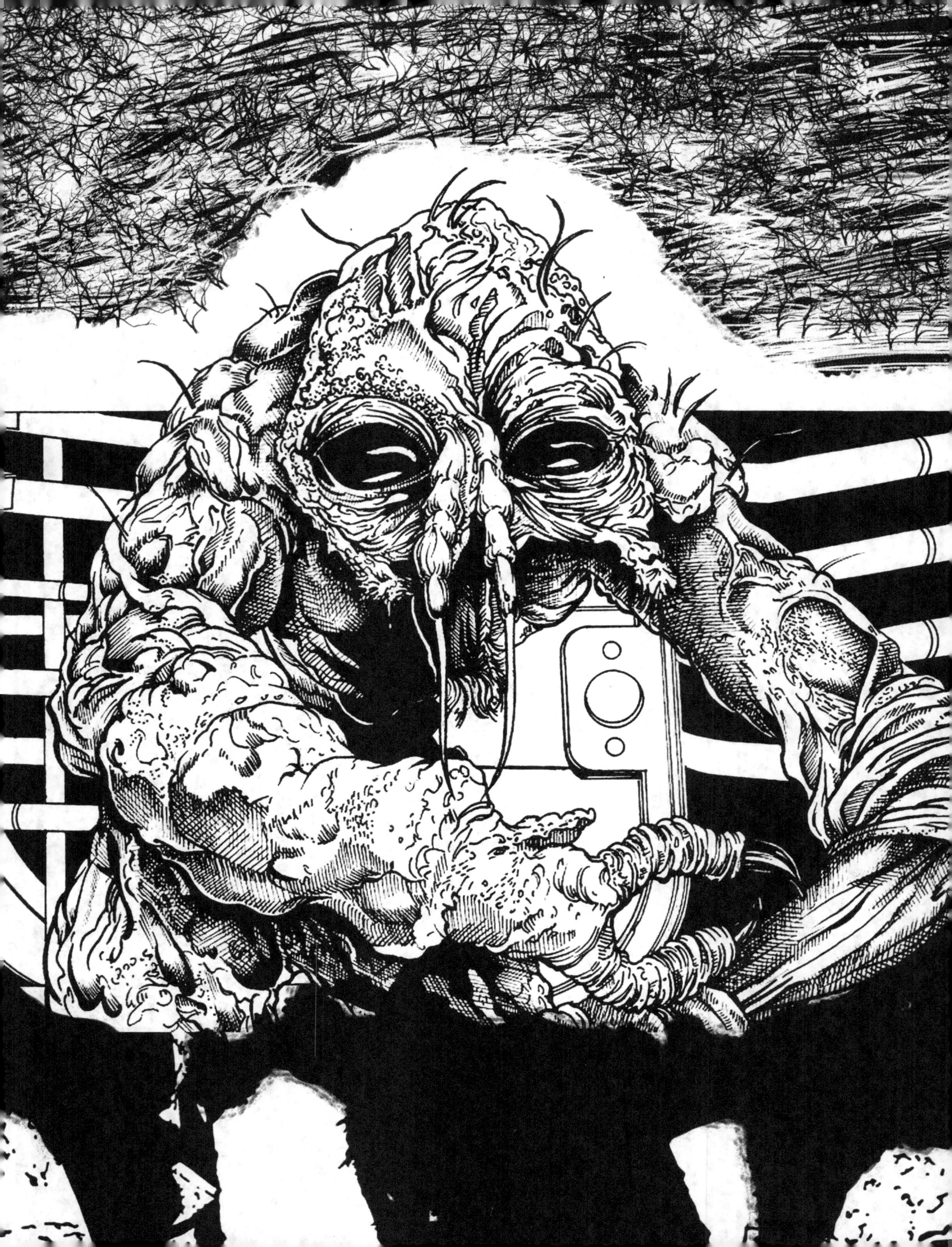

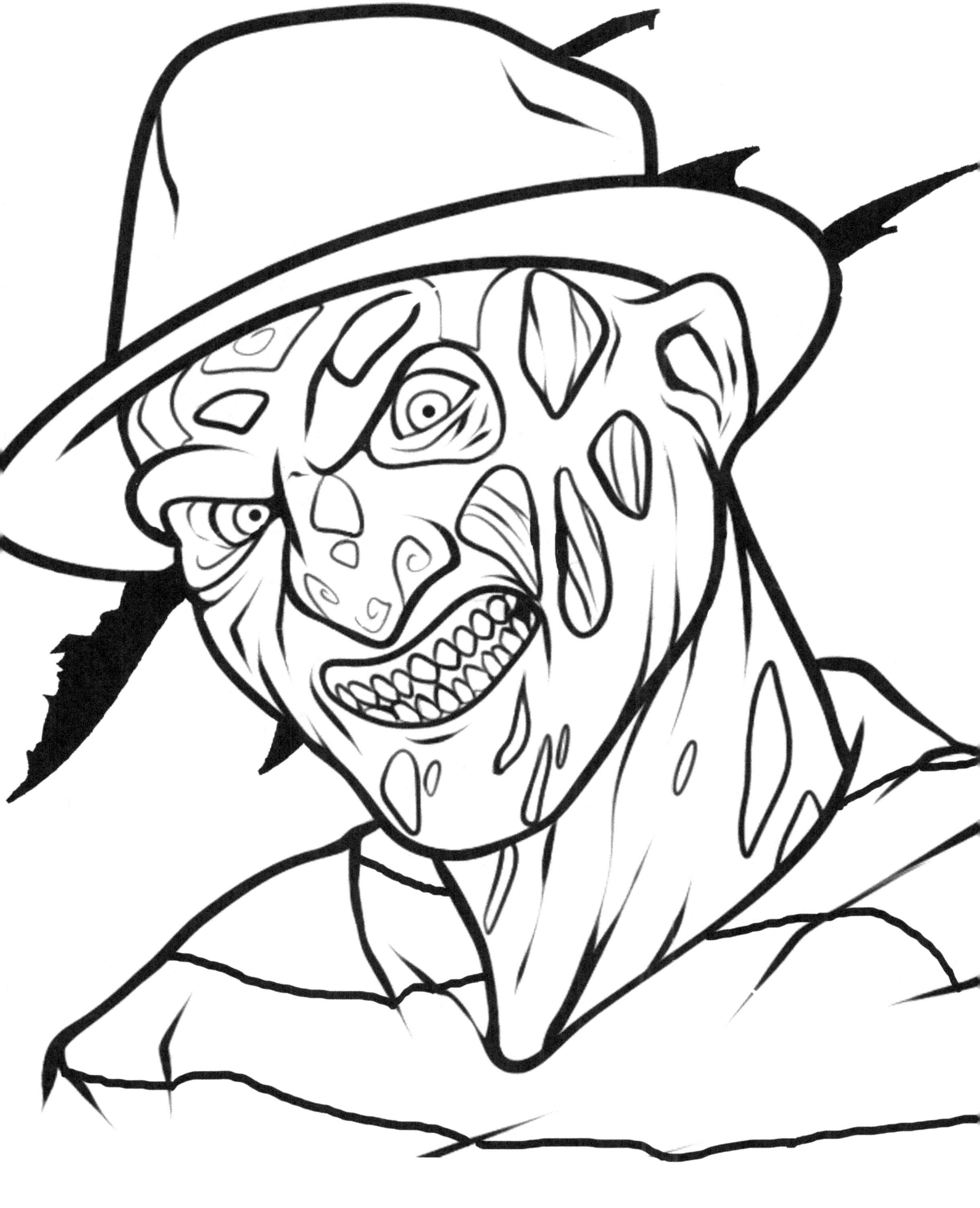

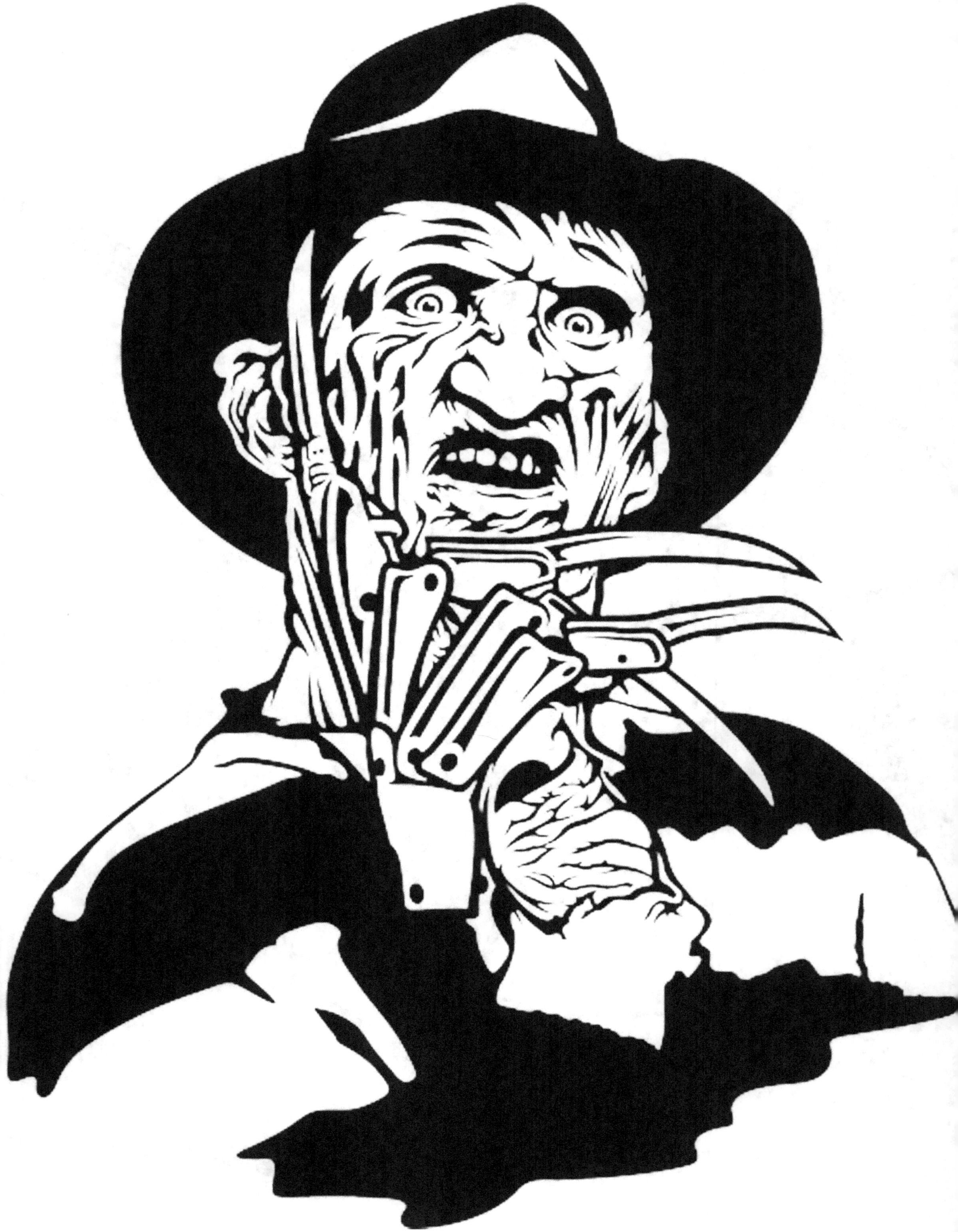

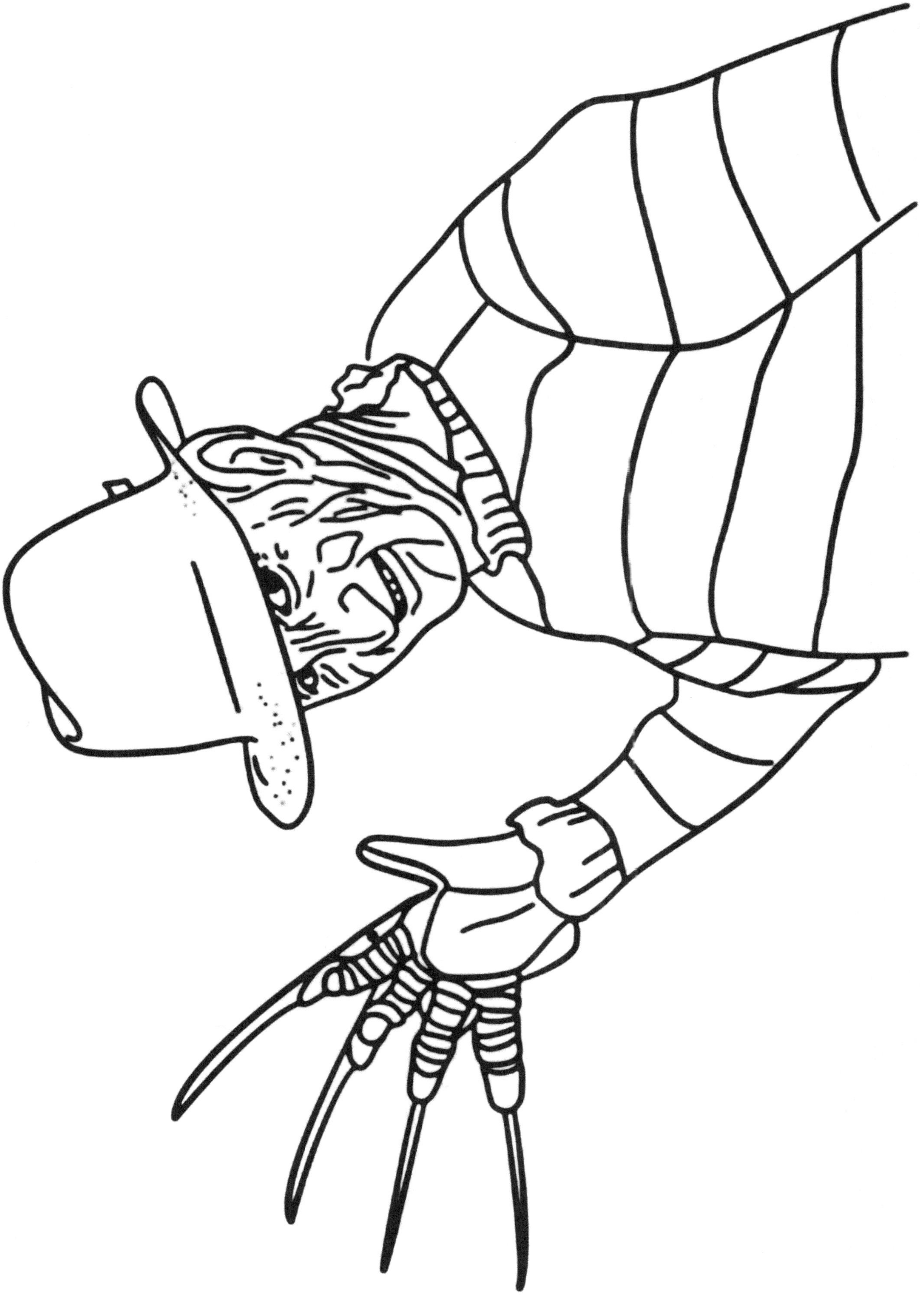

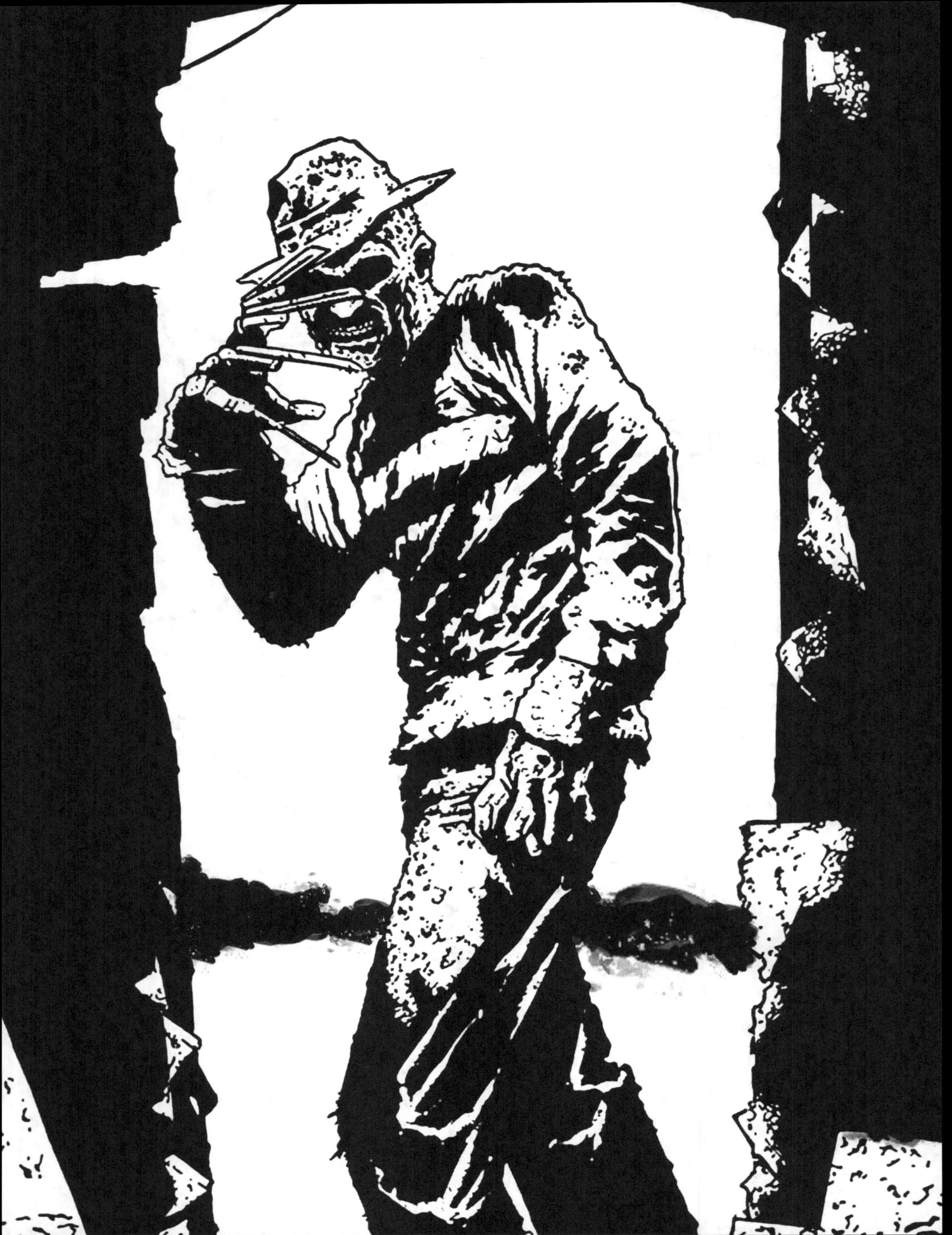

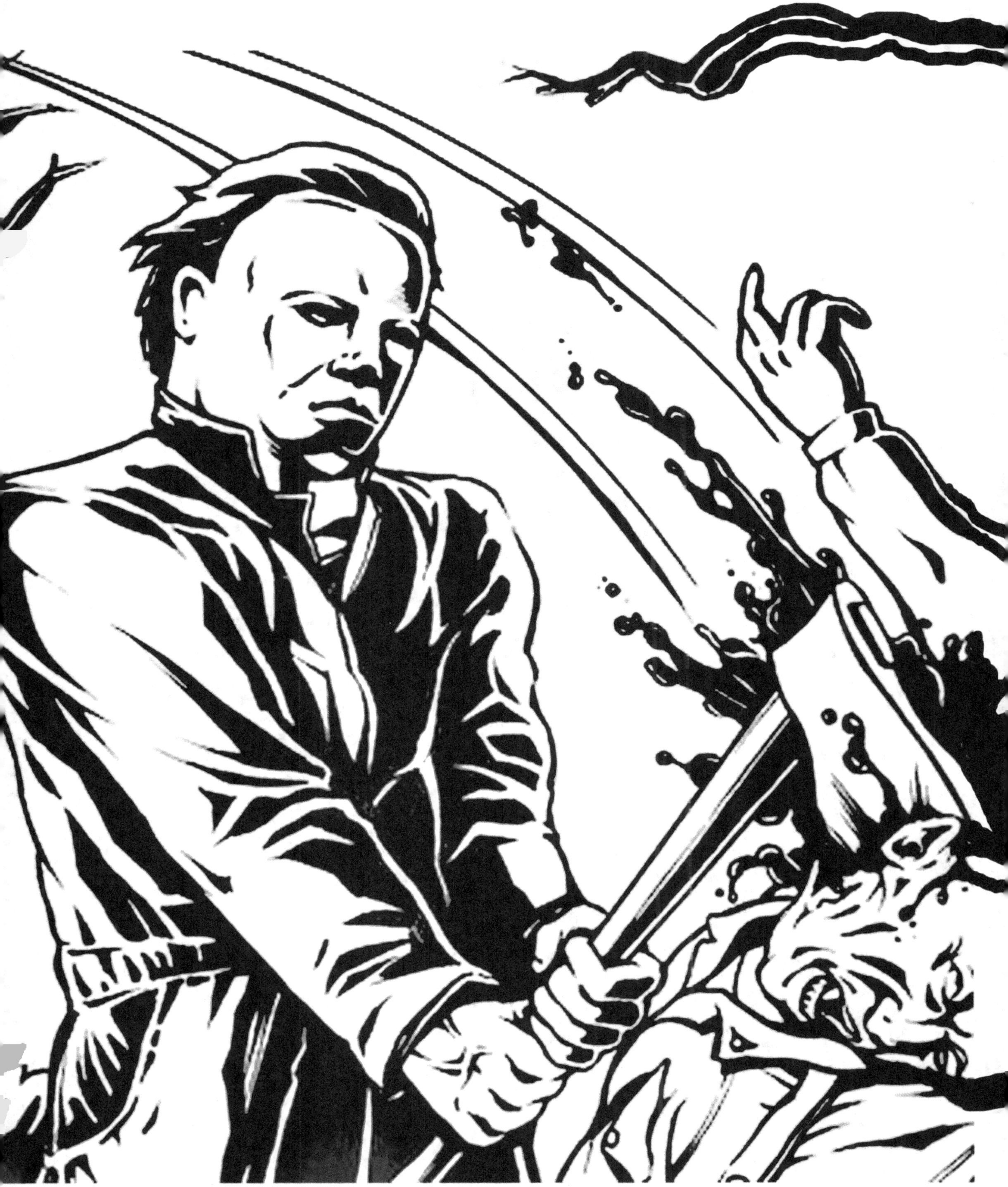

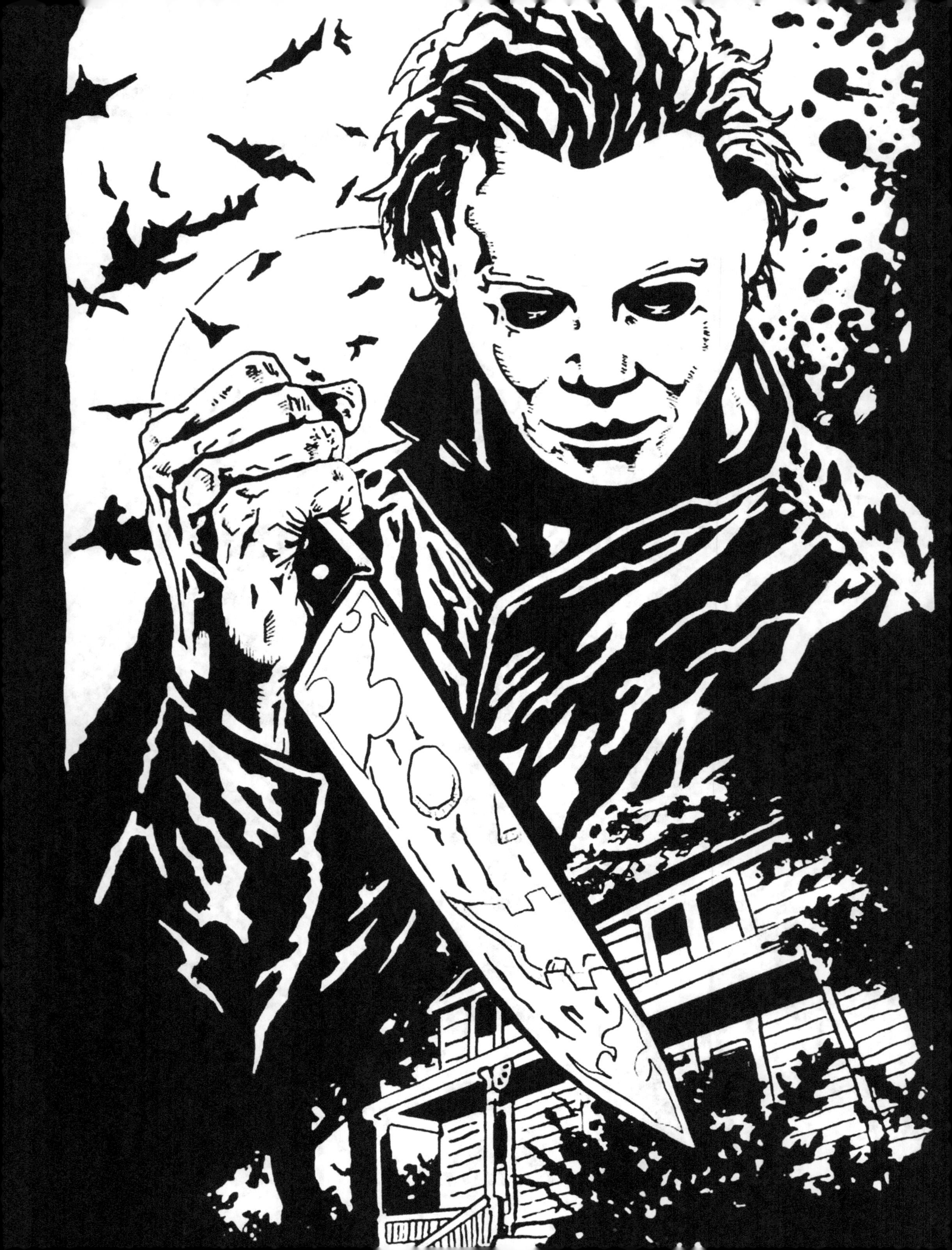

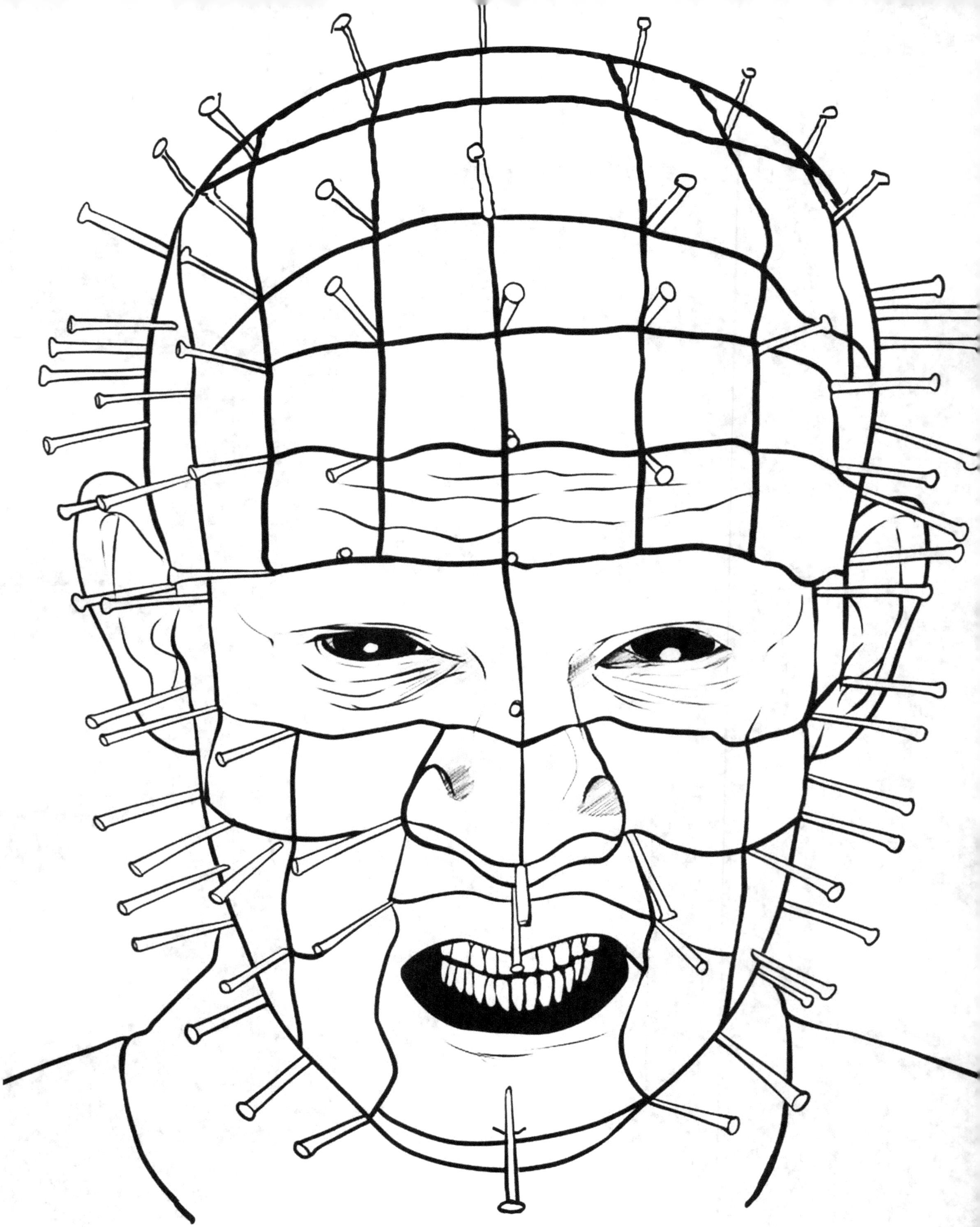

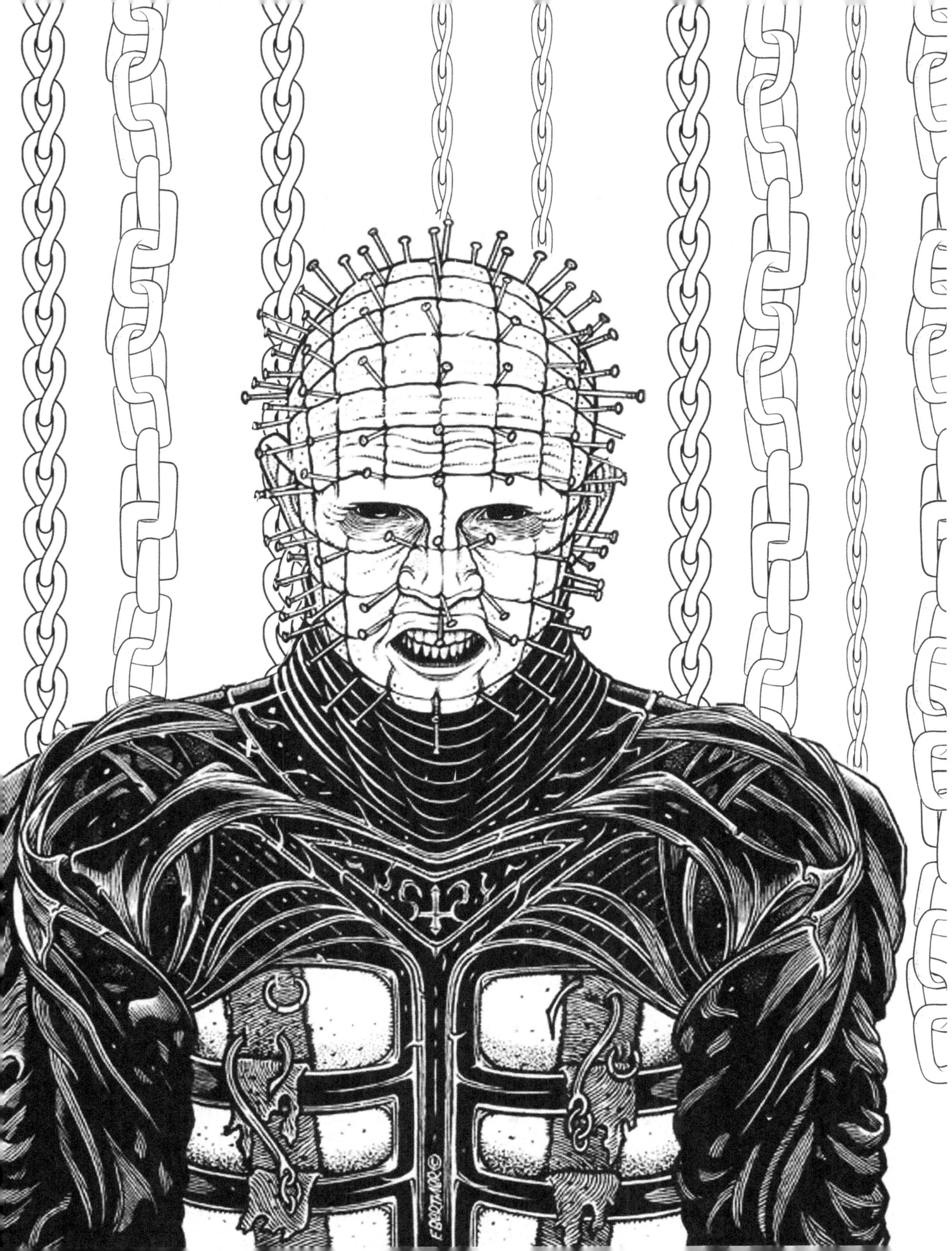

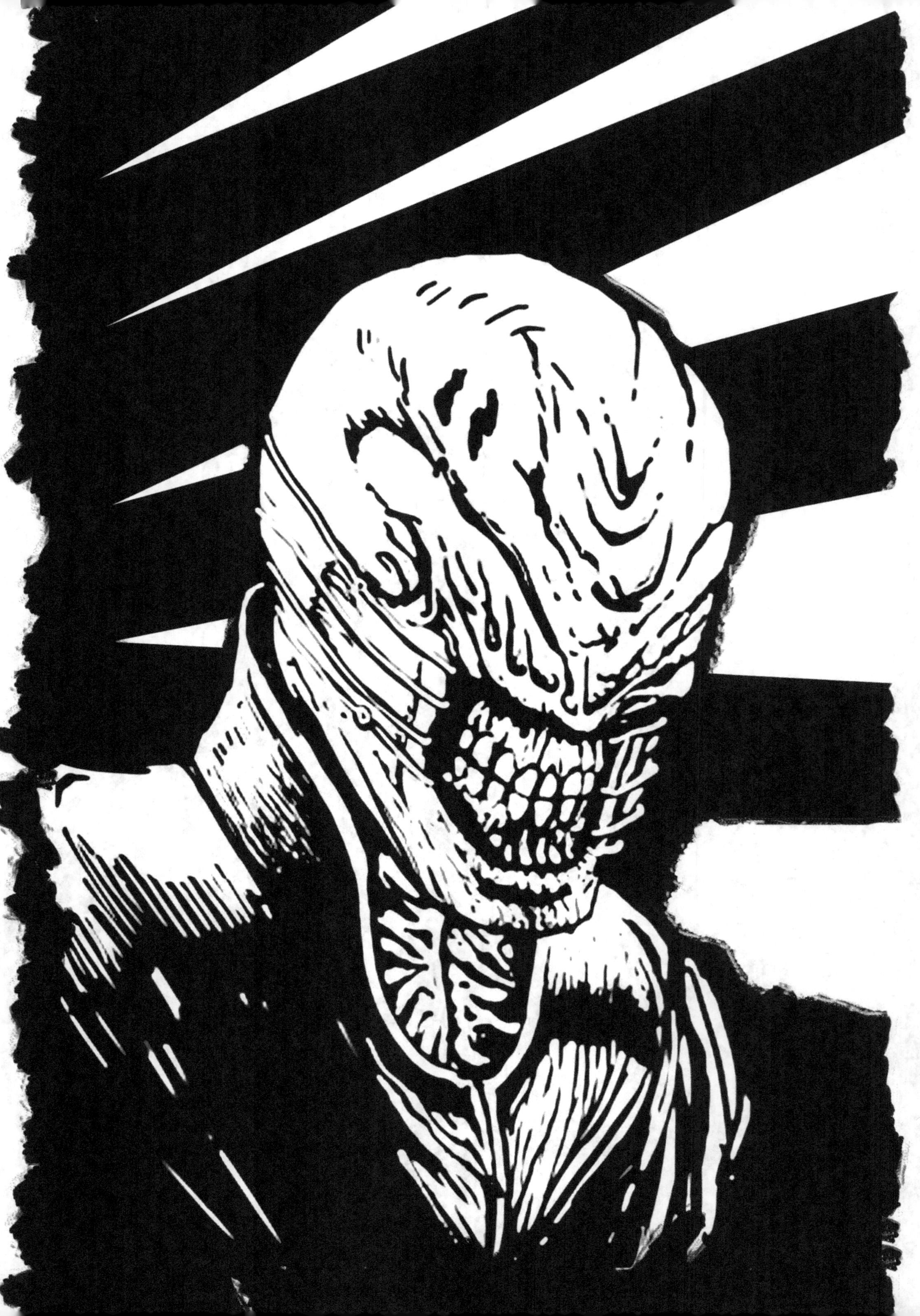

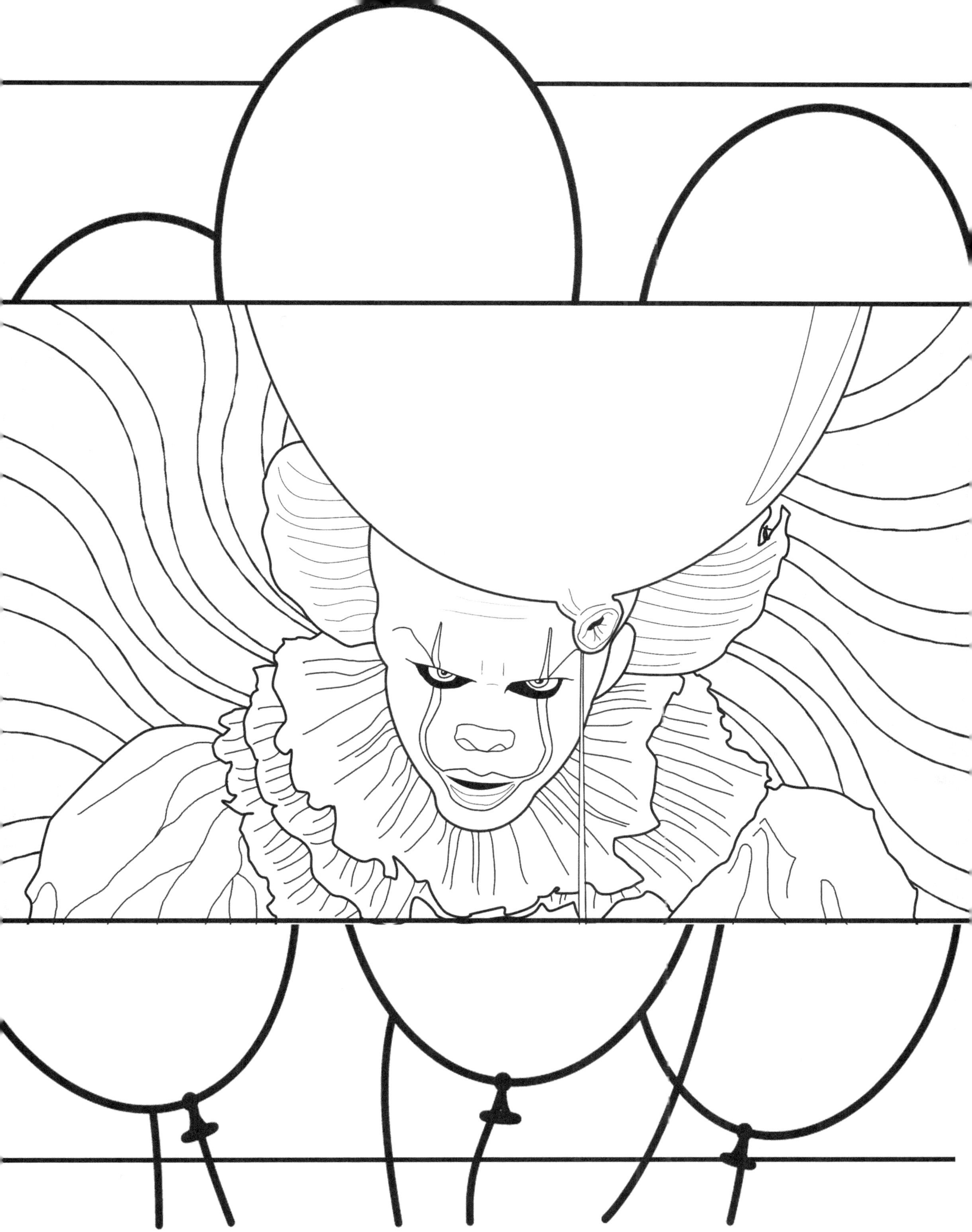

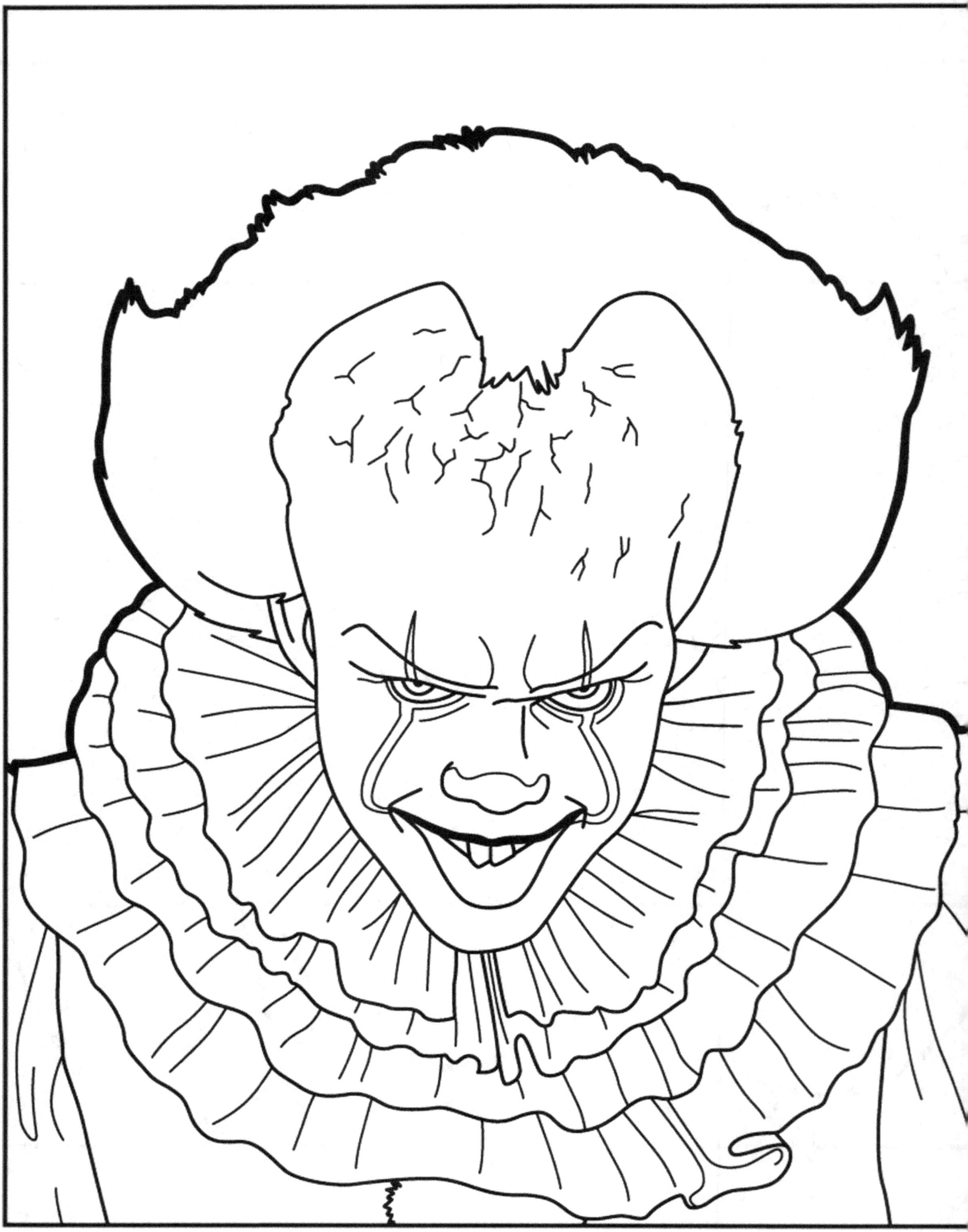

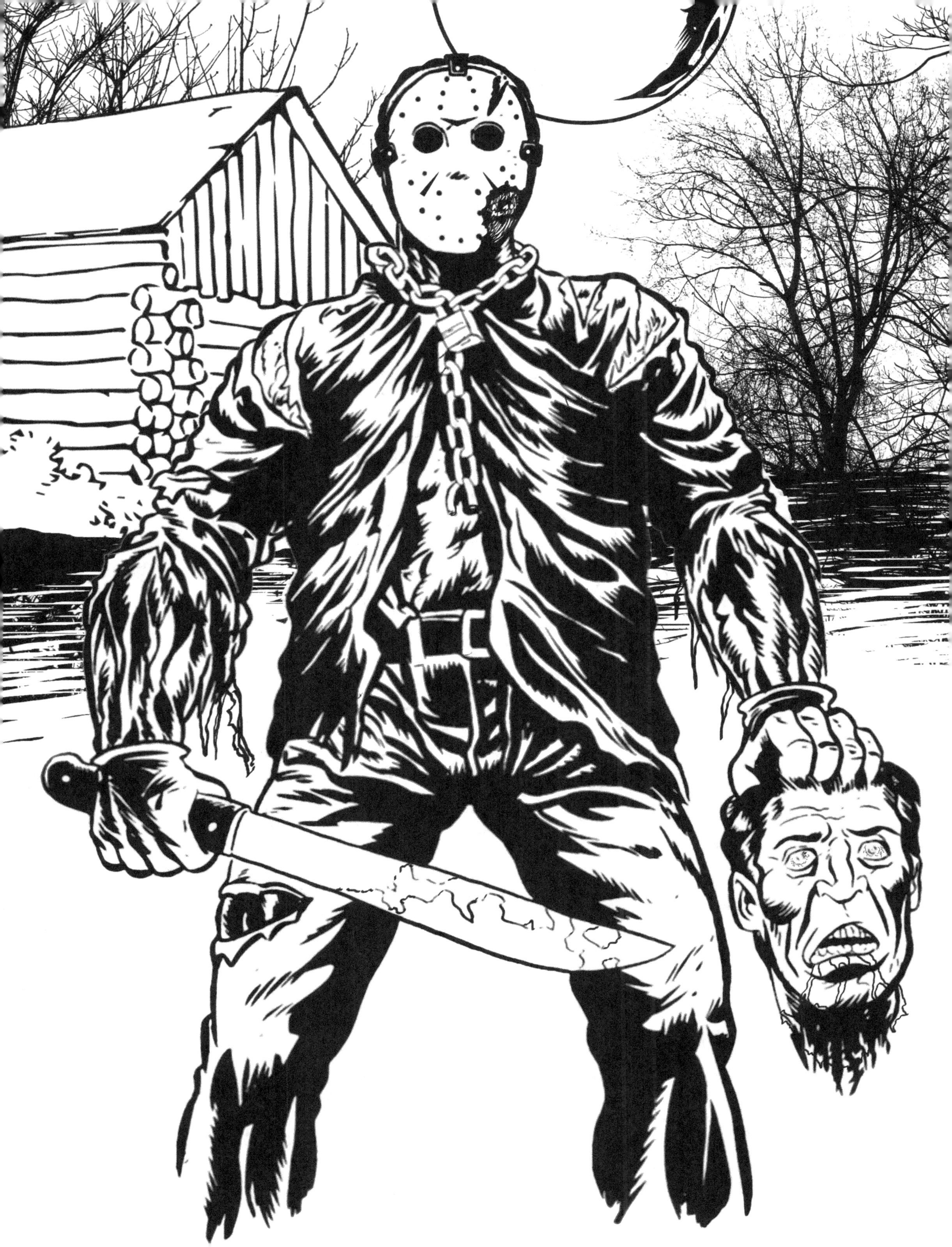

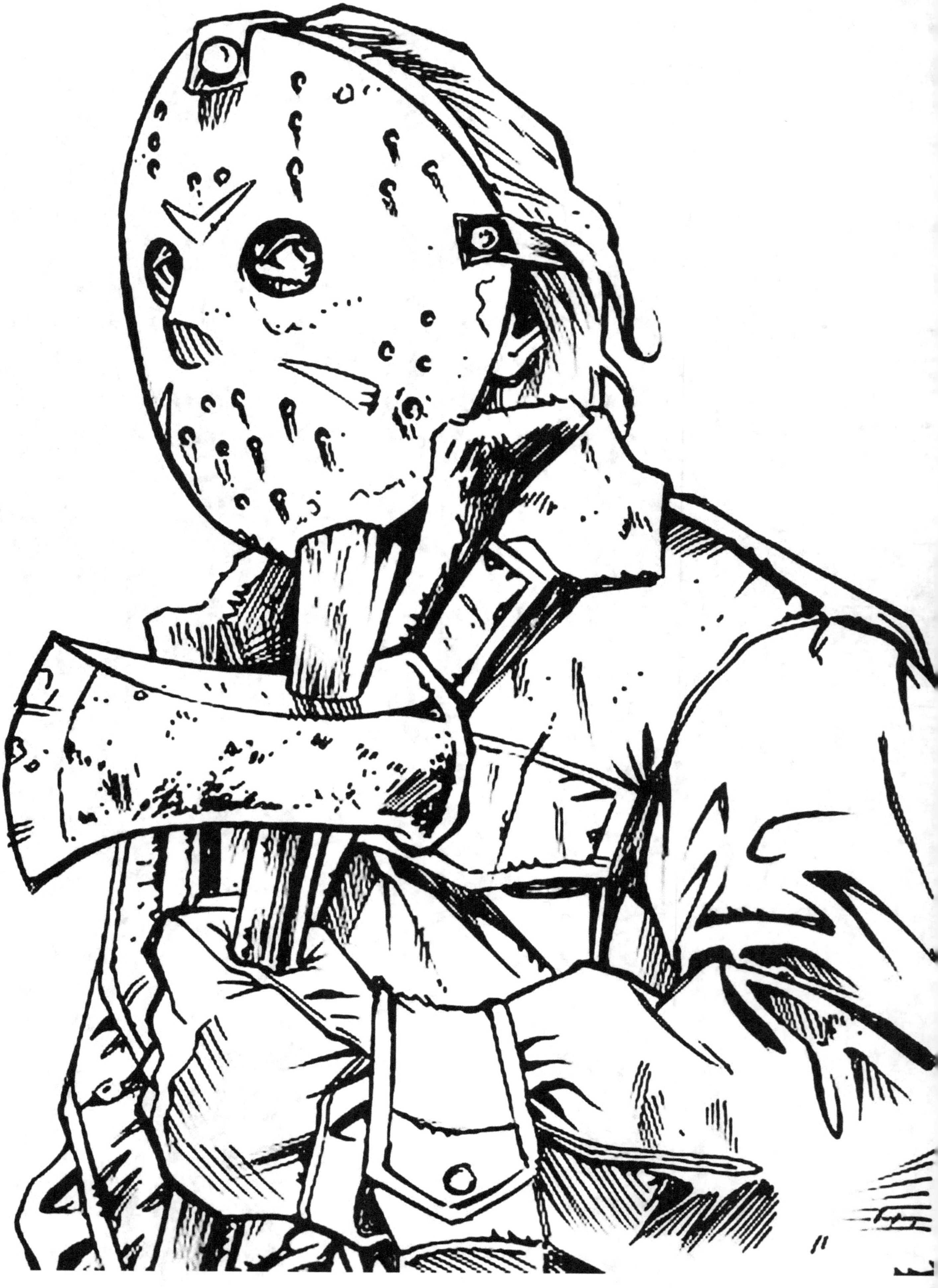

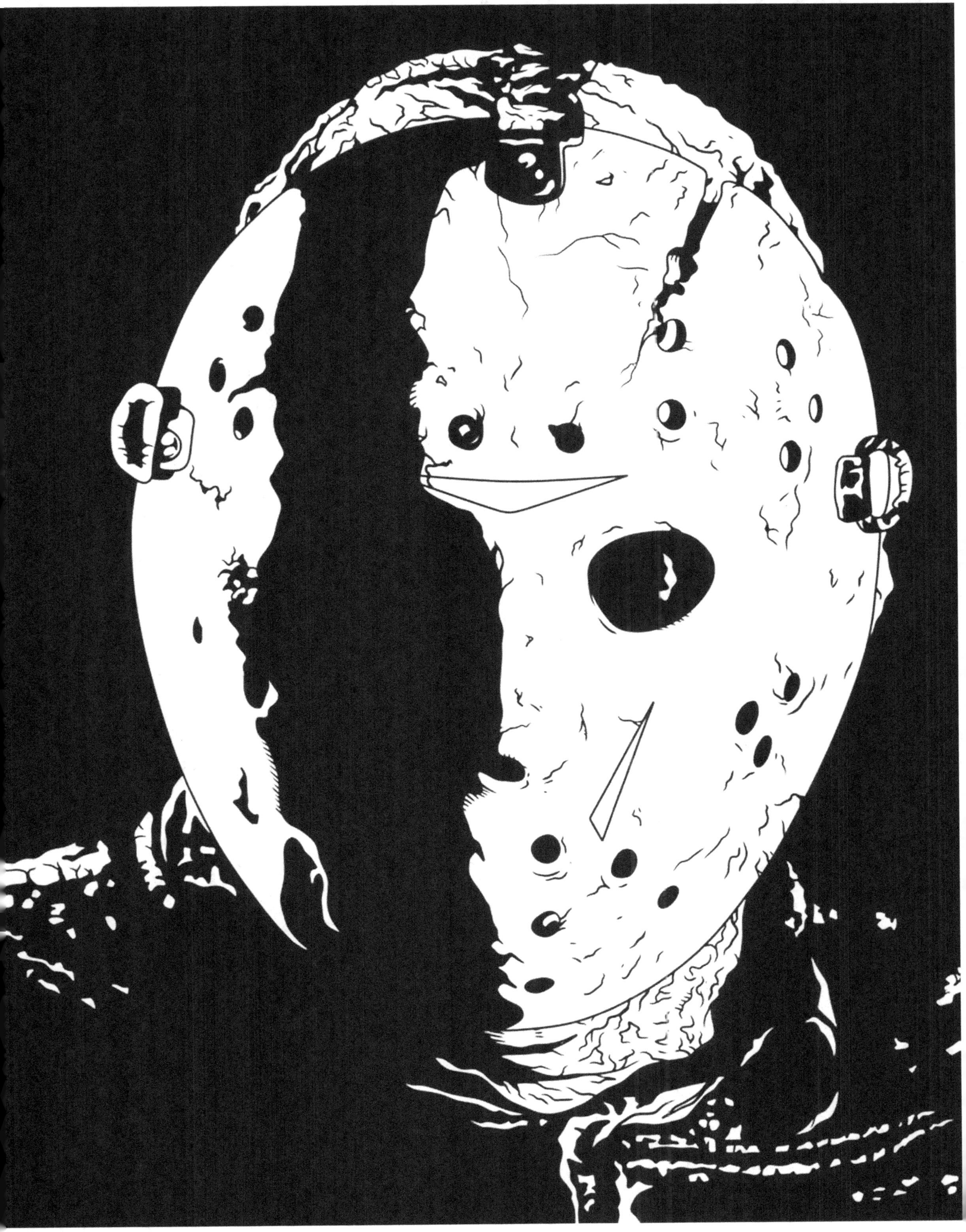

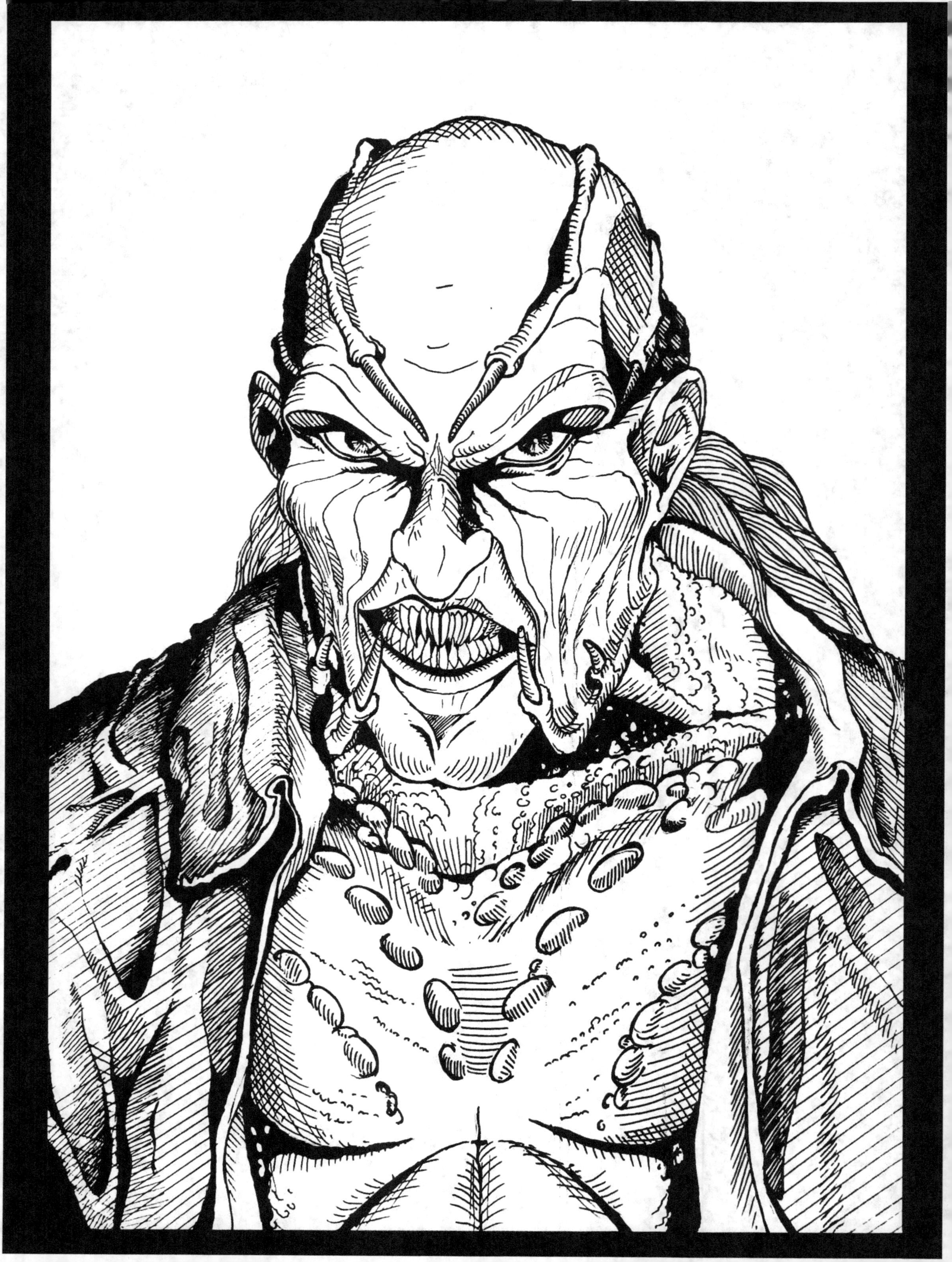

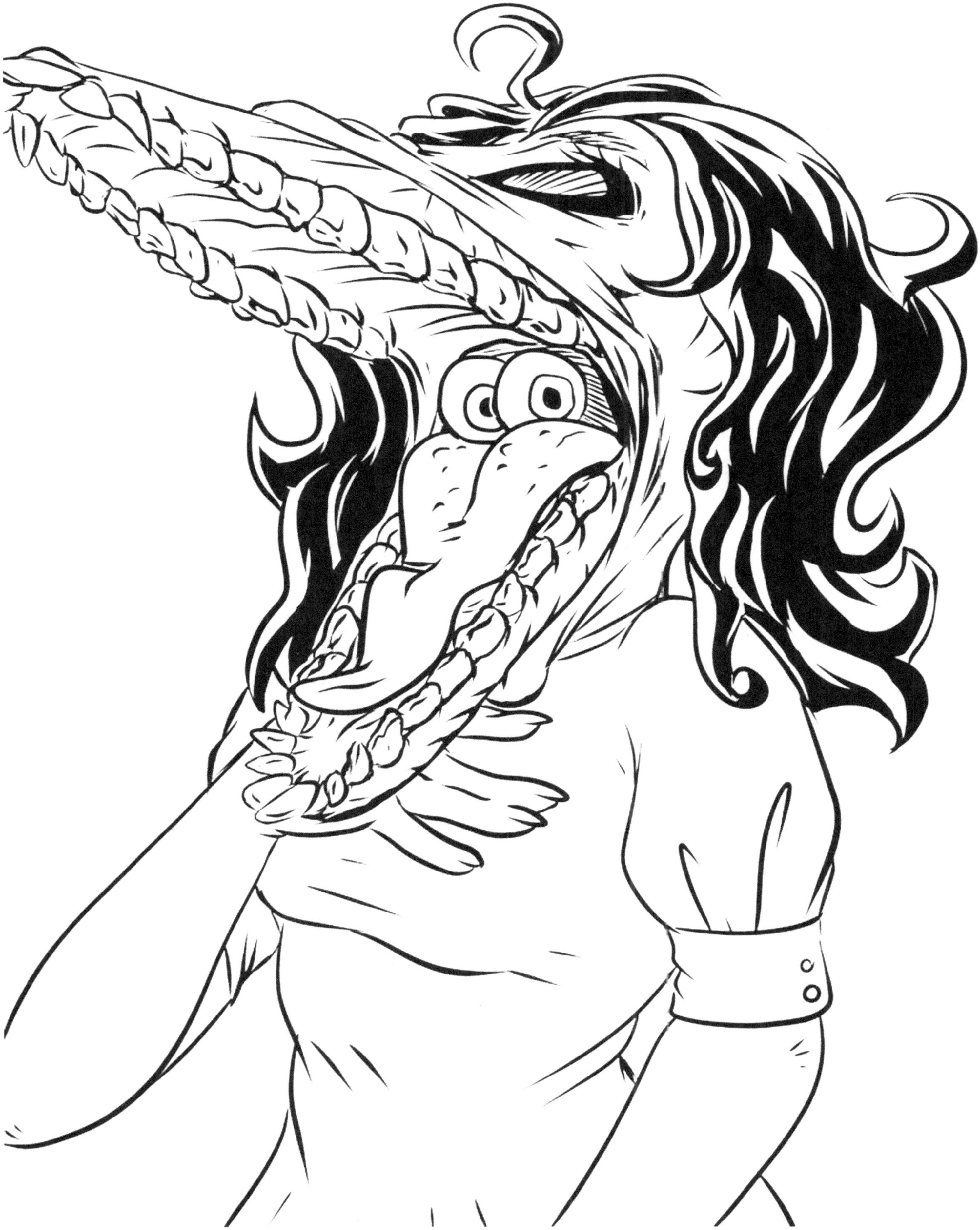

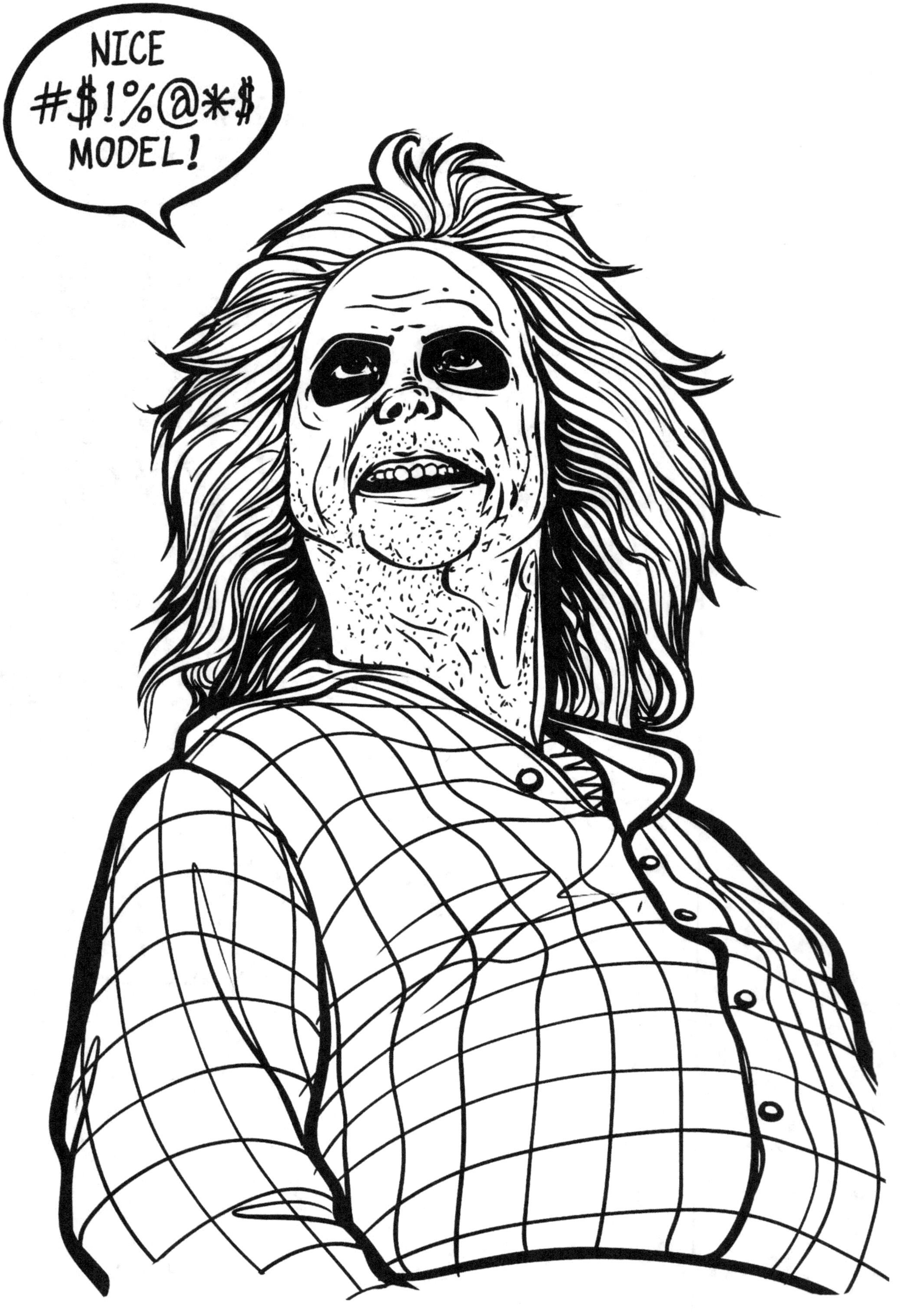
NICE
#$!%@*$
MODEL!

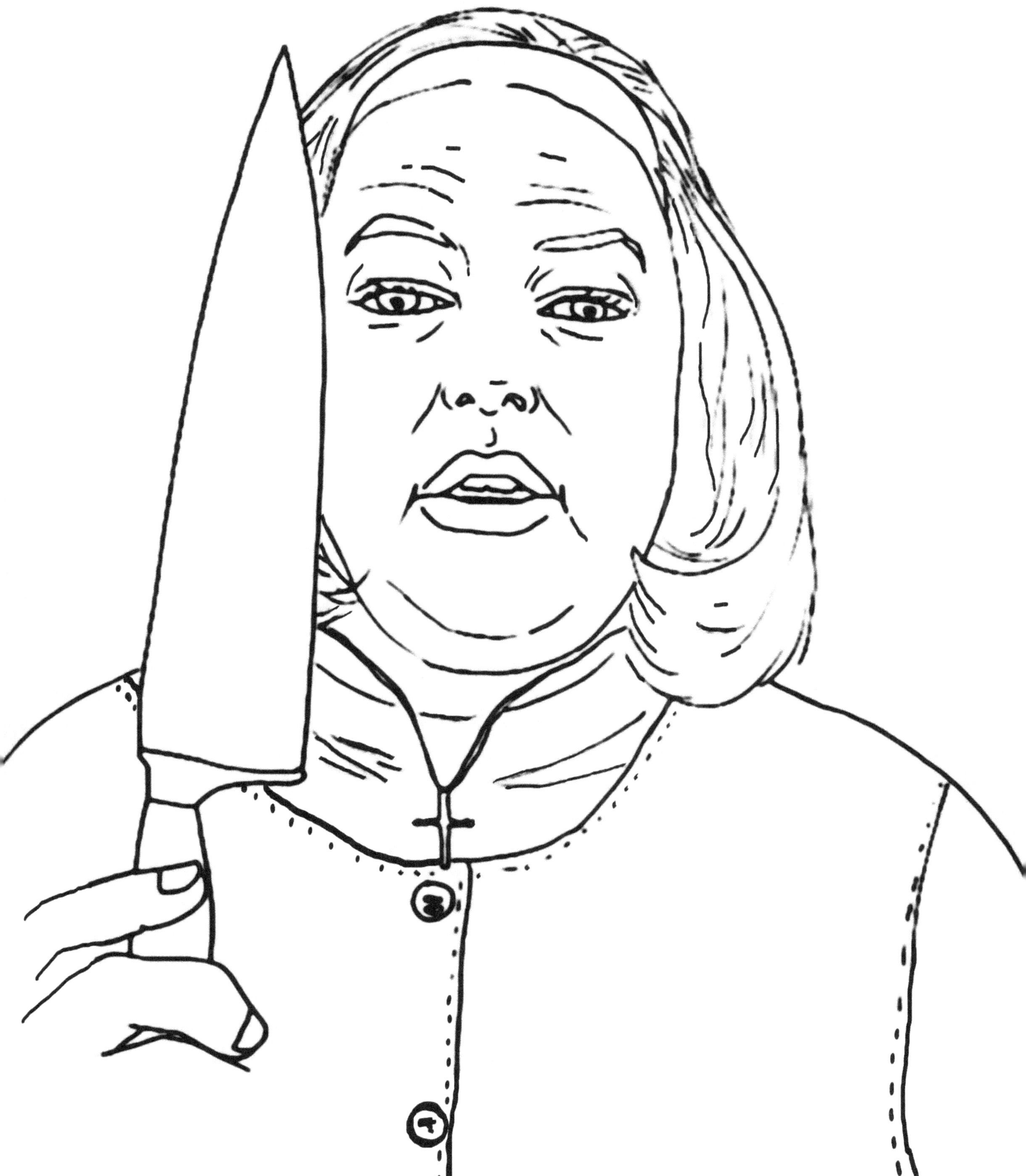

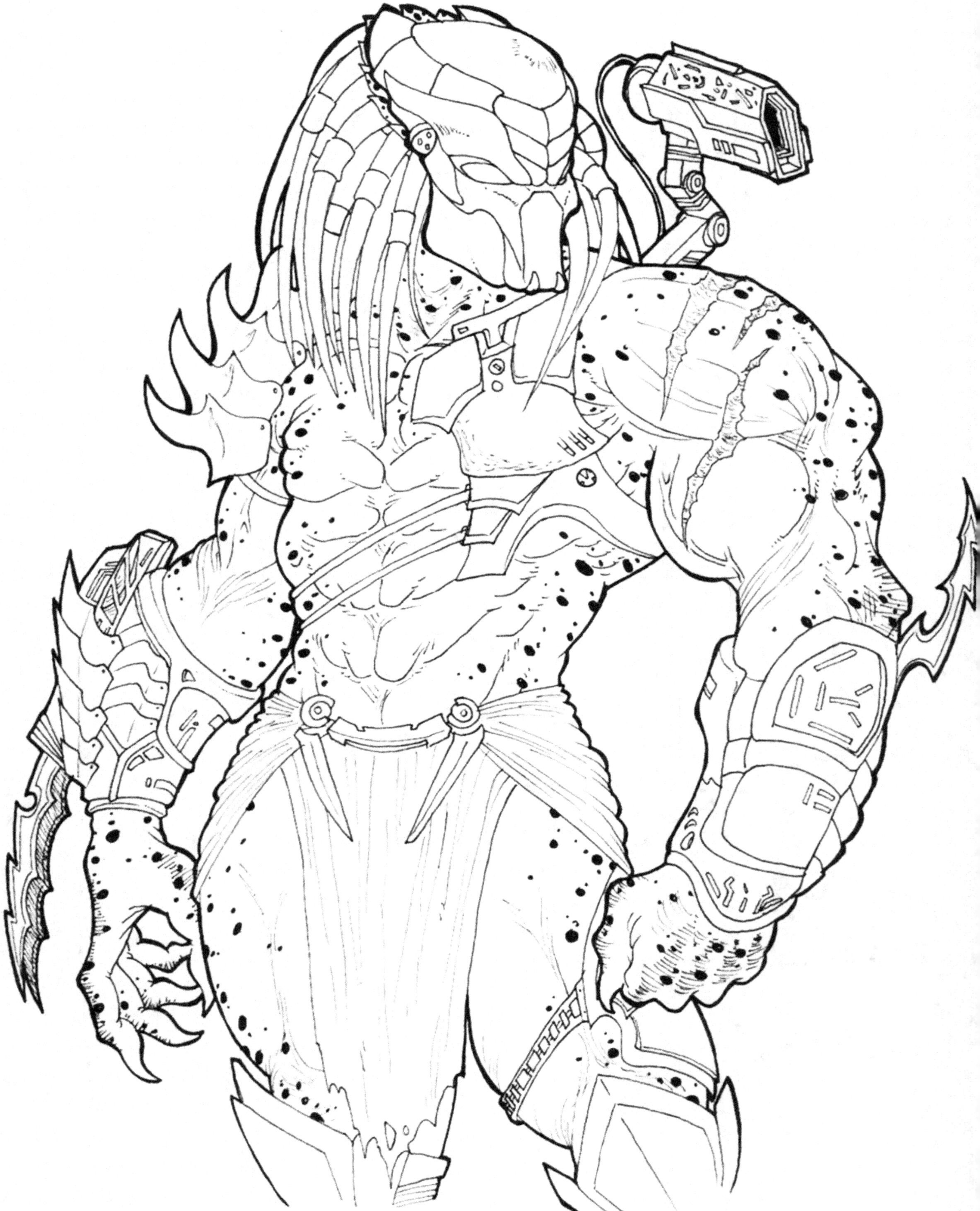

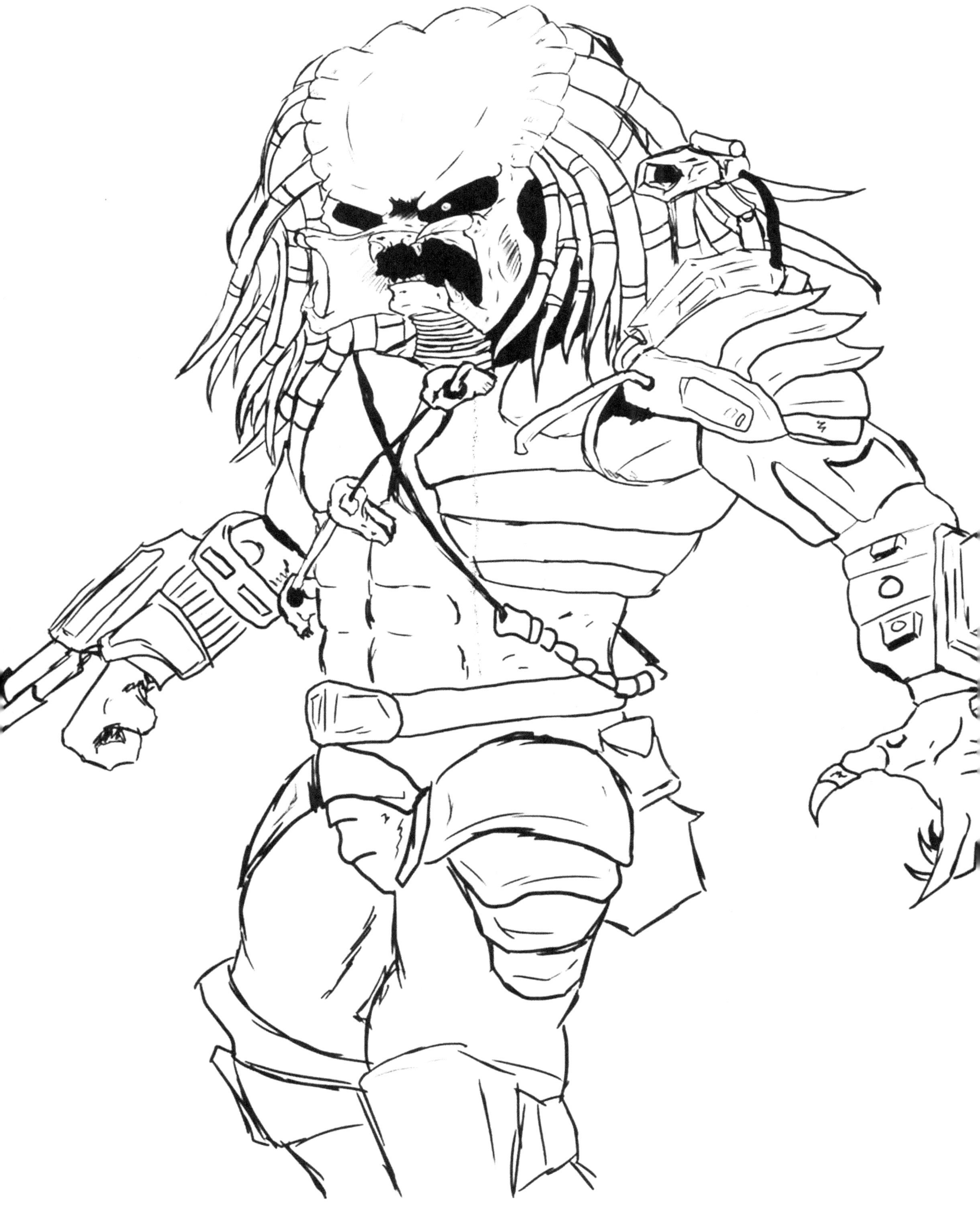

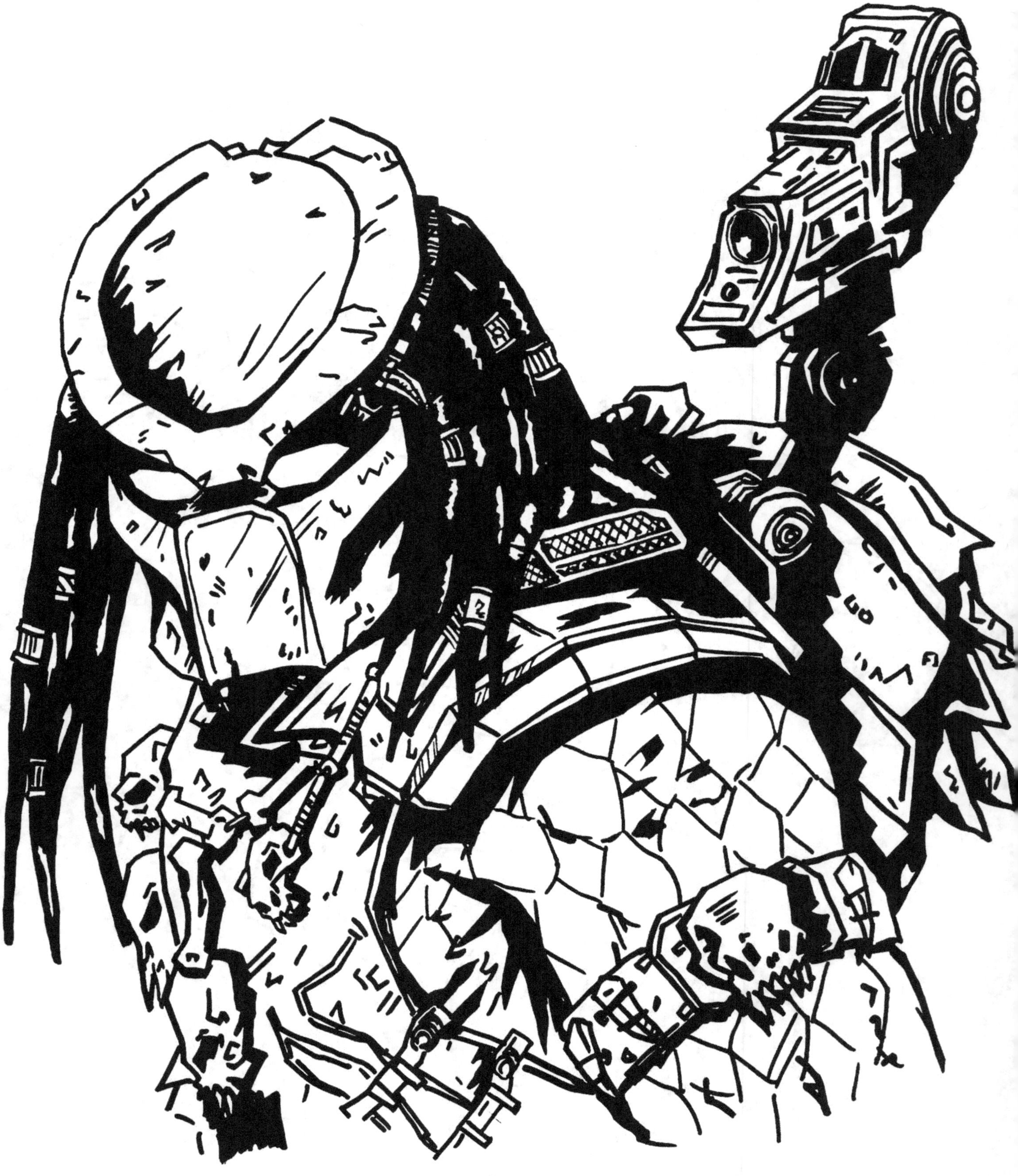

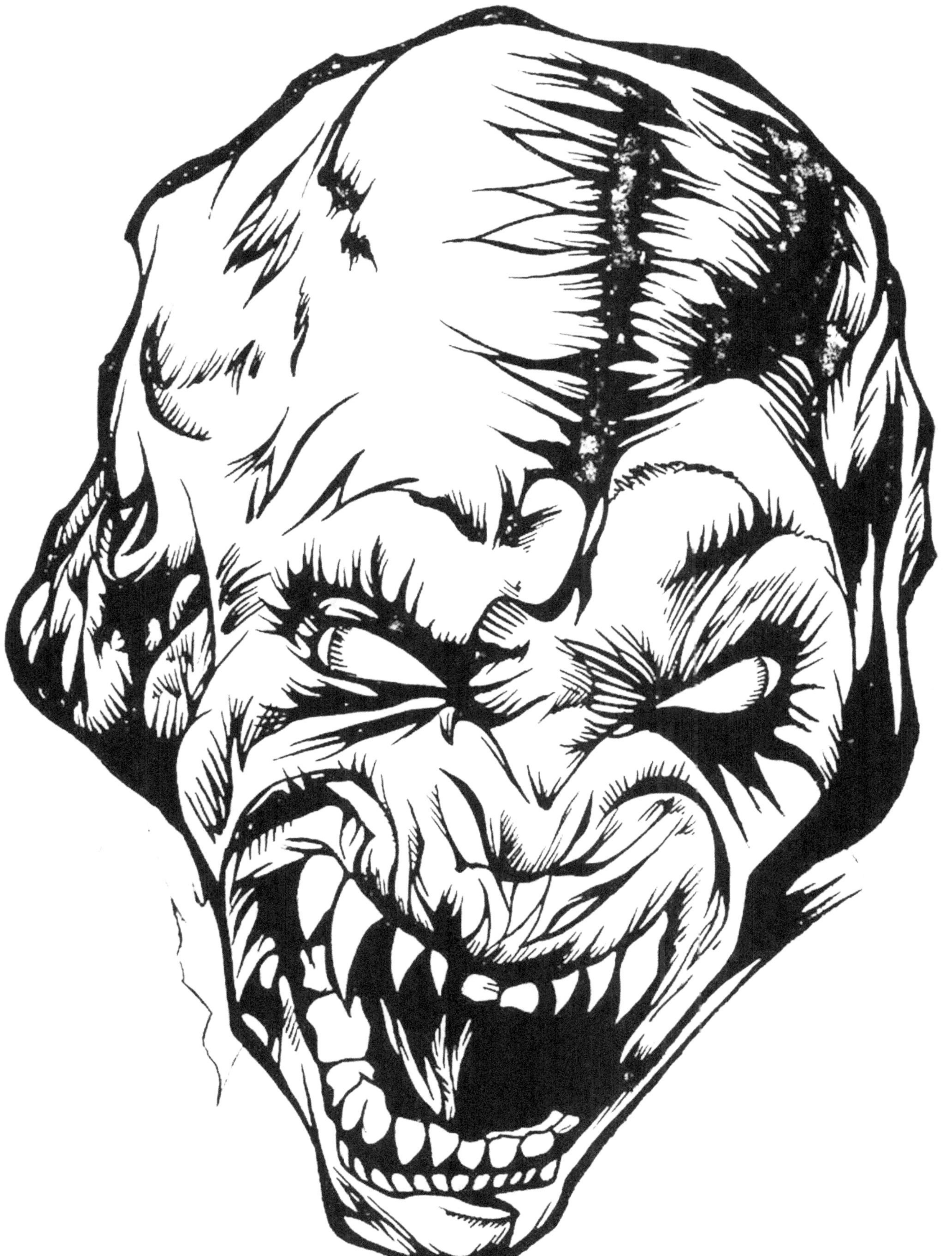

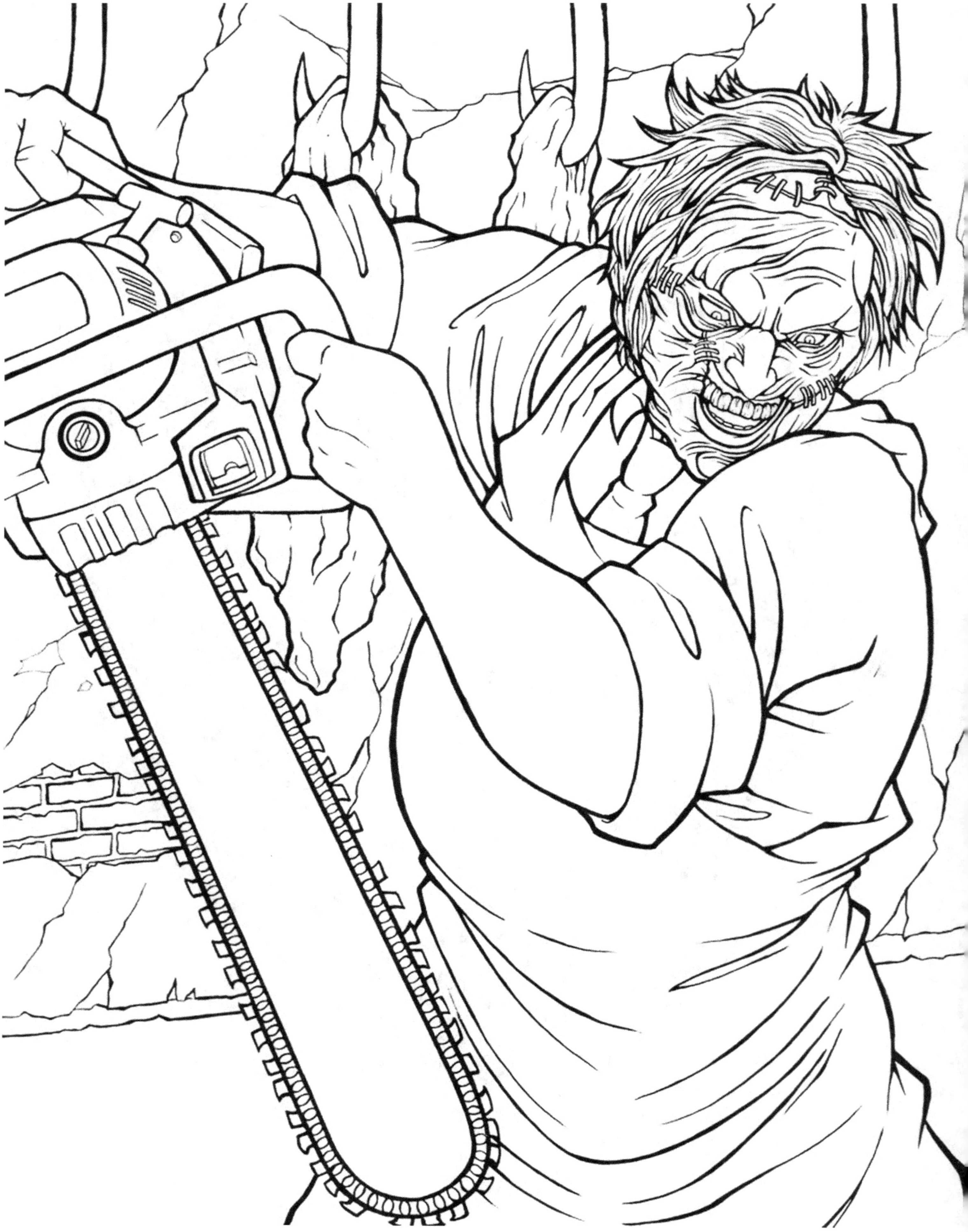

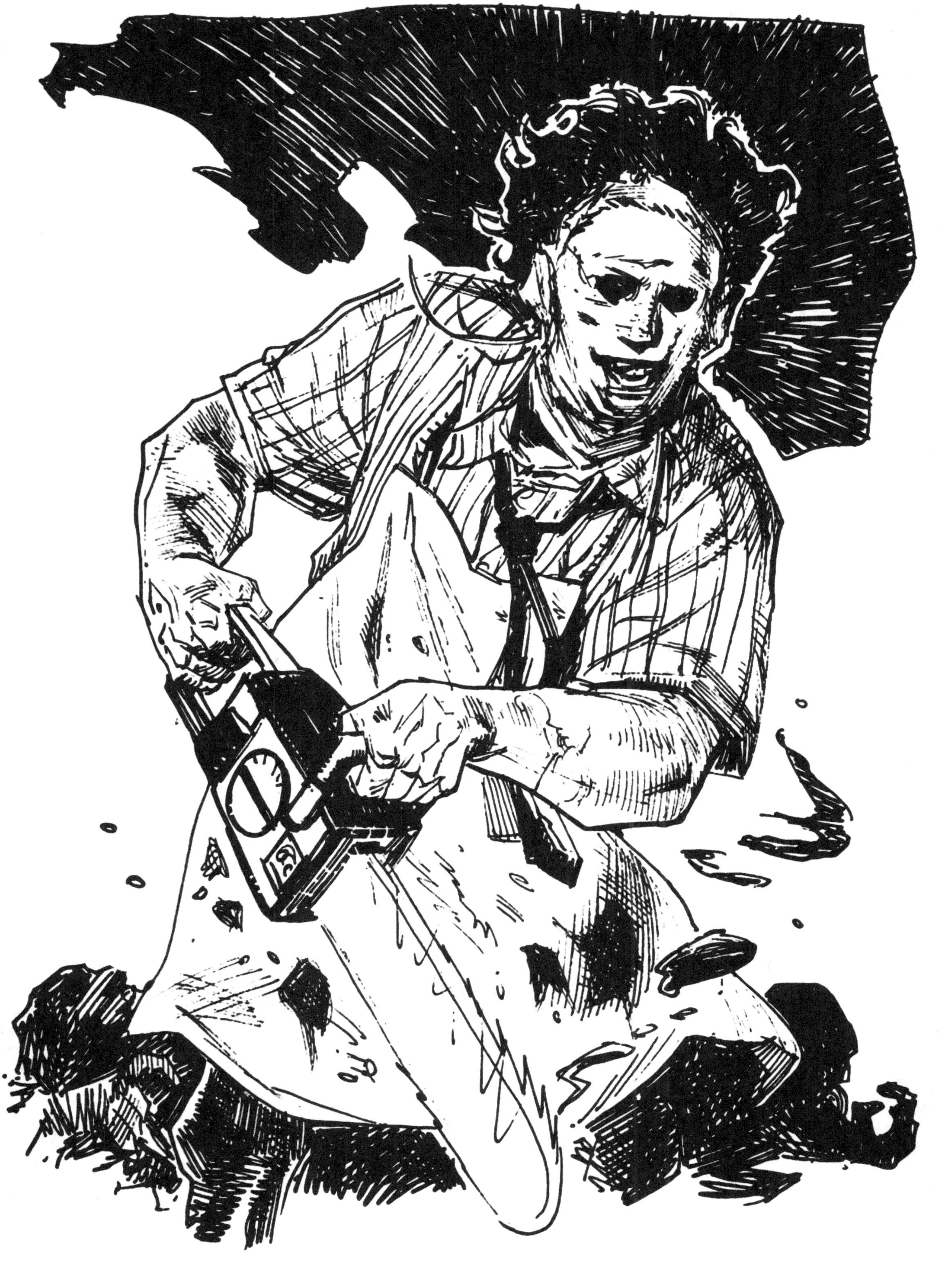

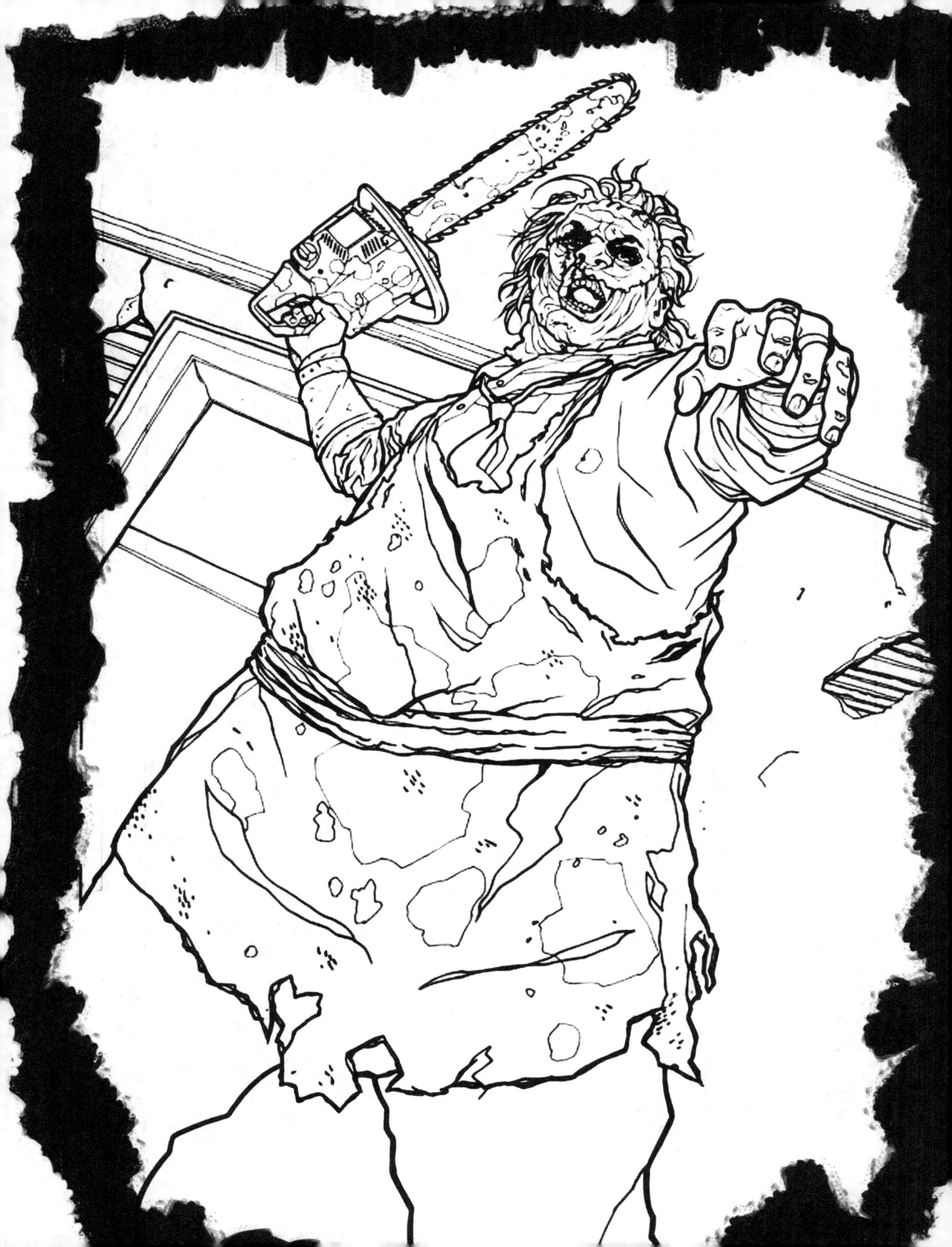

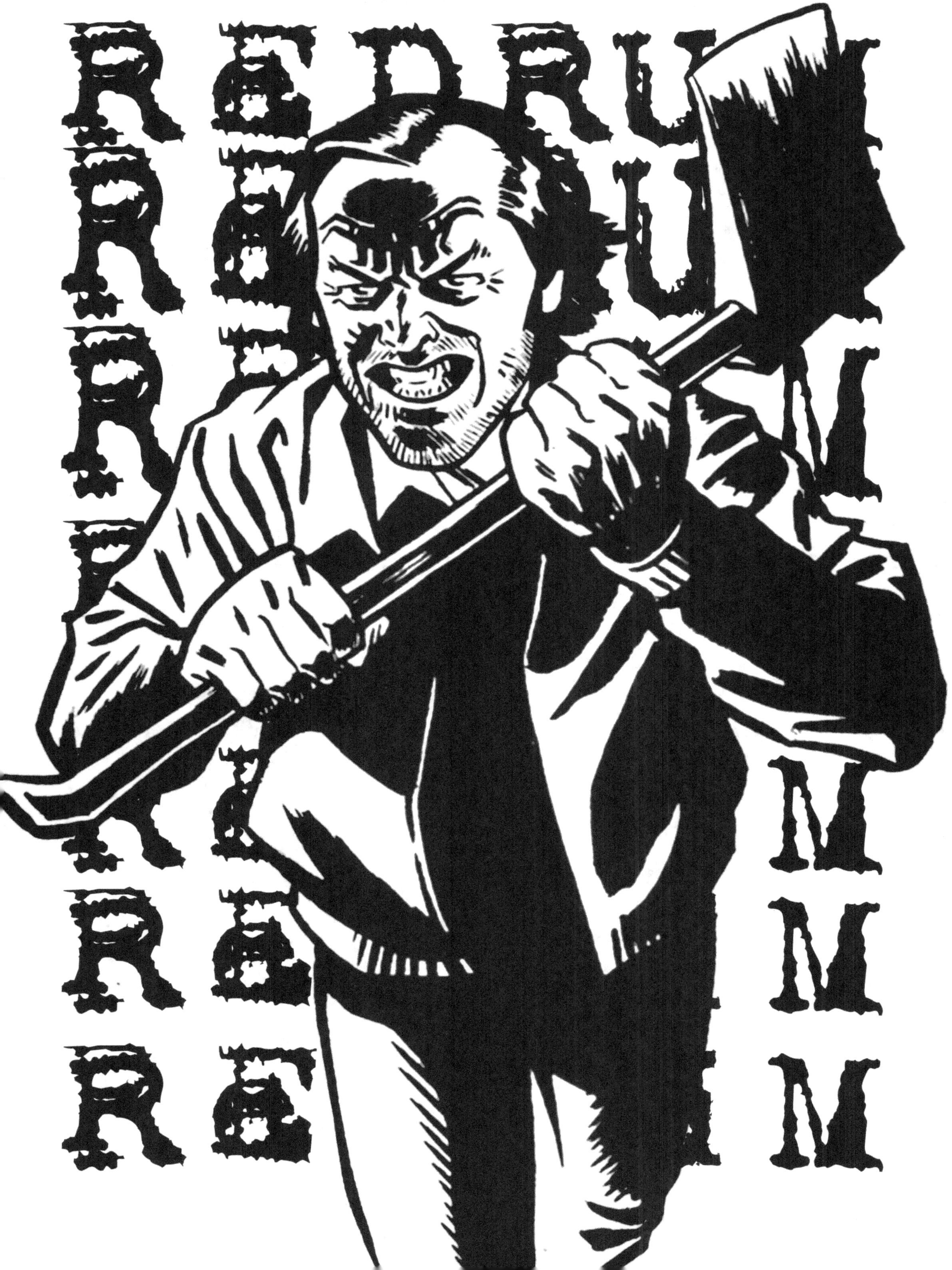
REDRUM

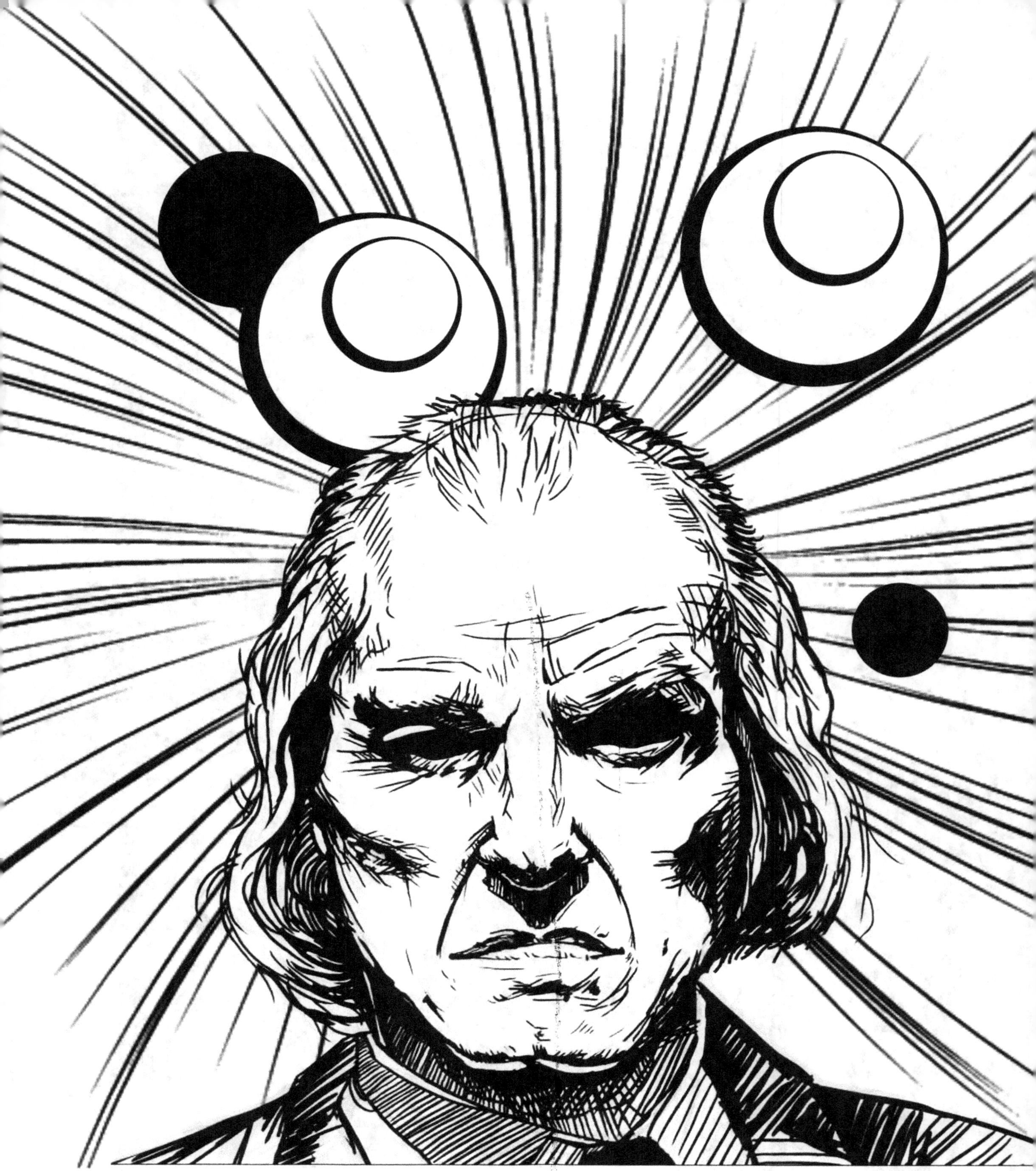

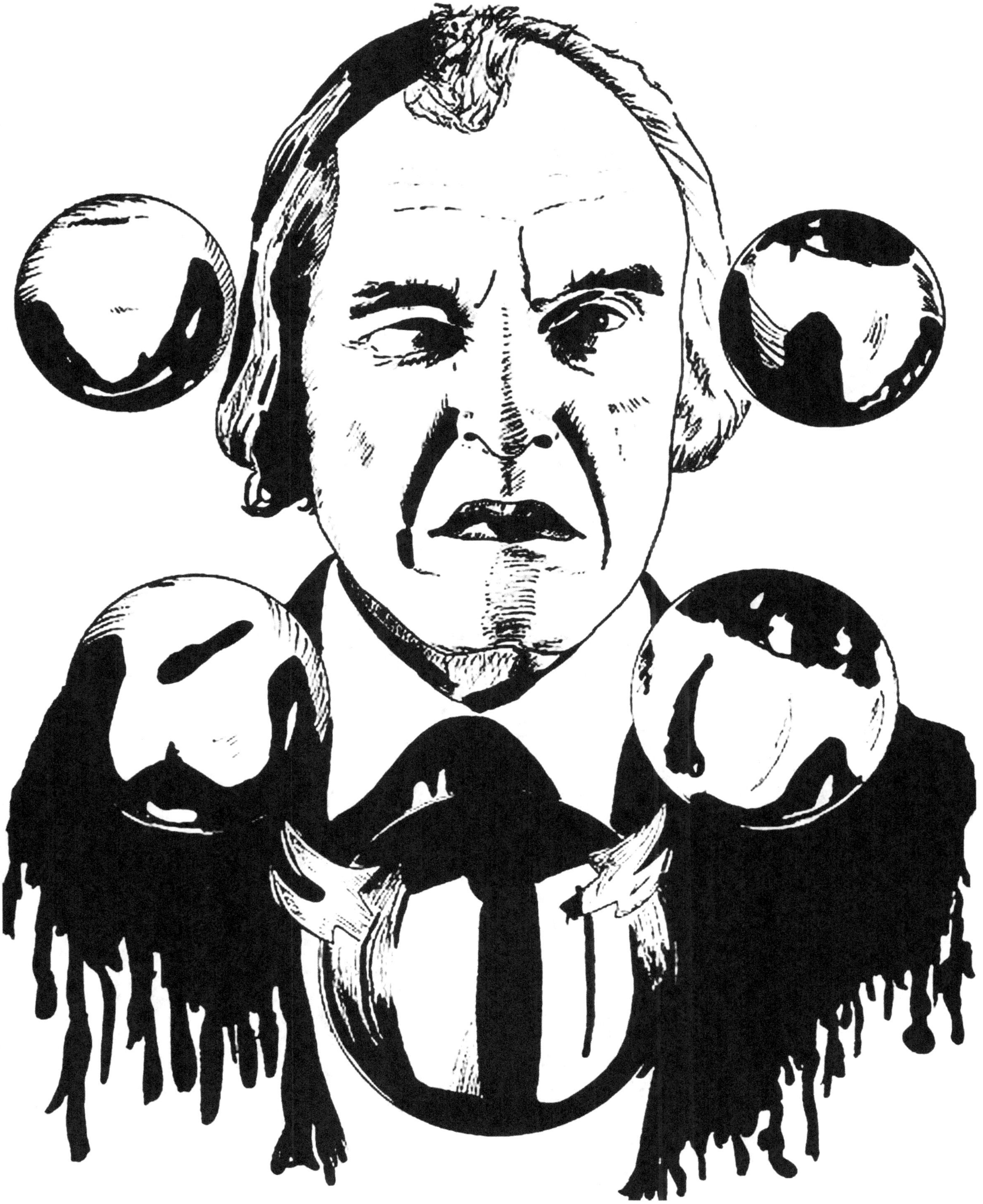

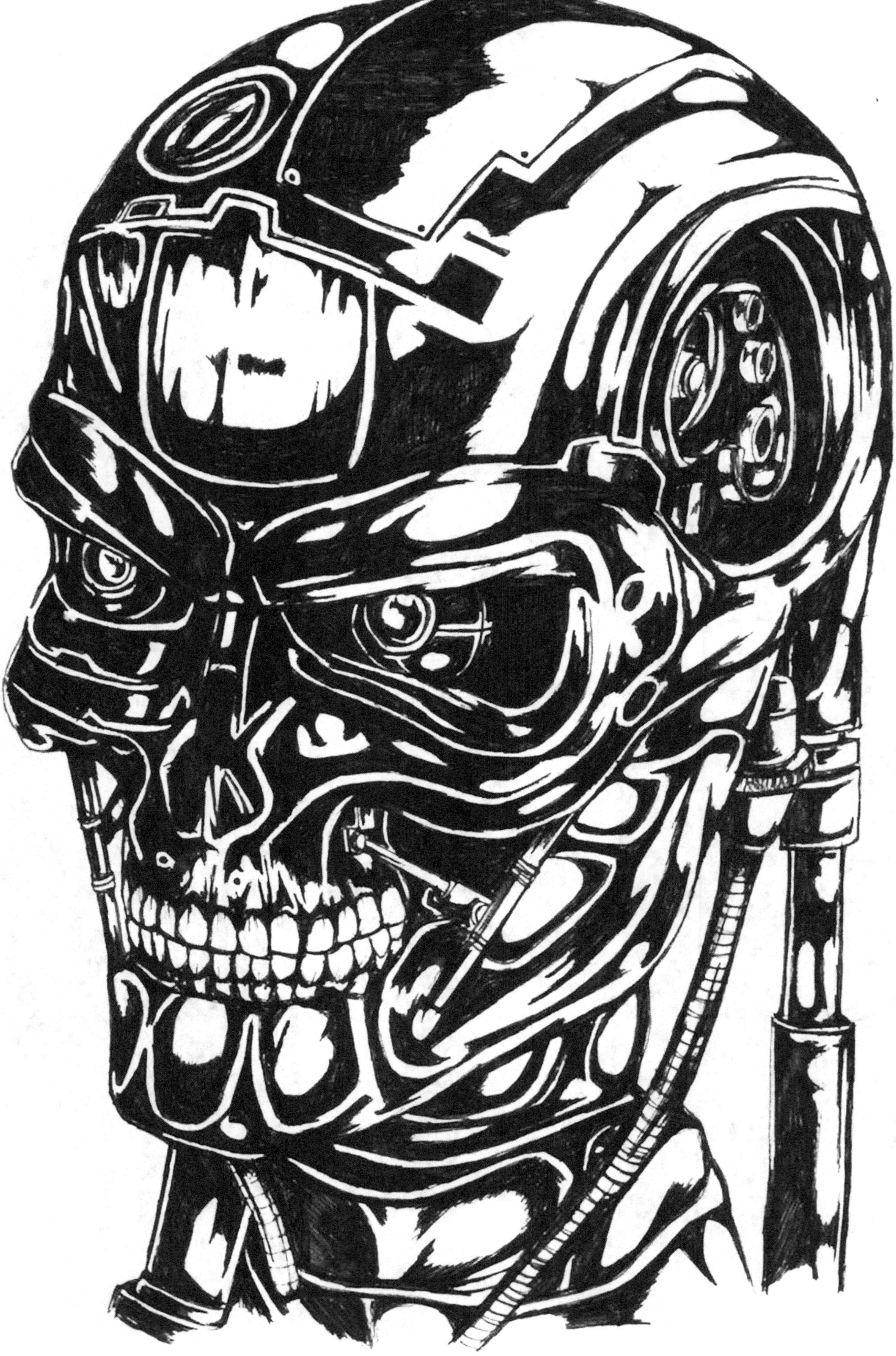

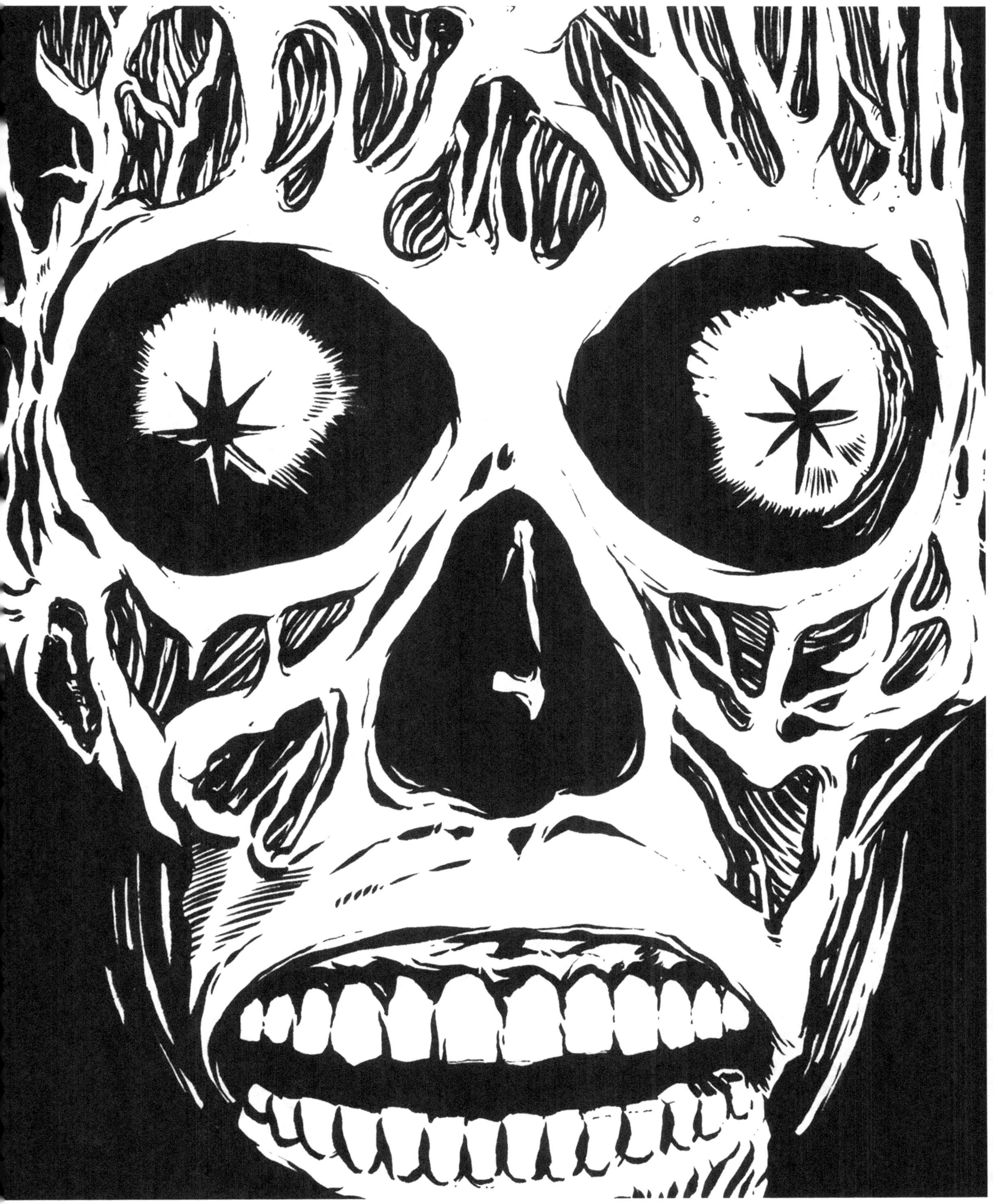

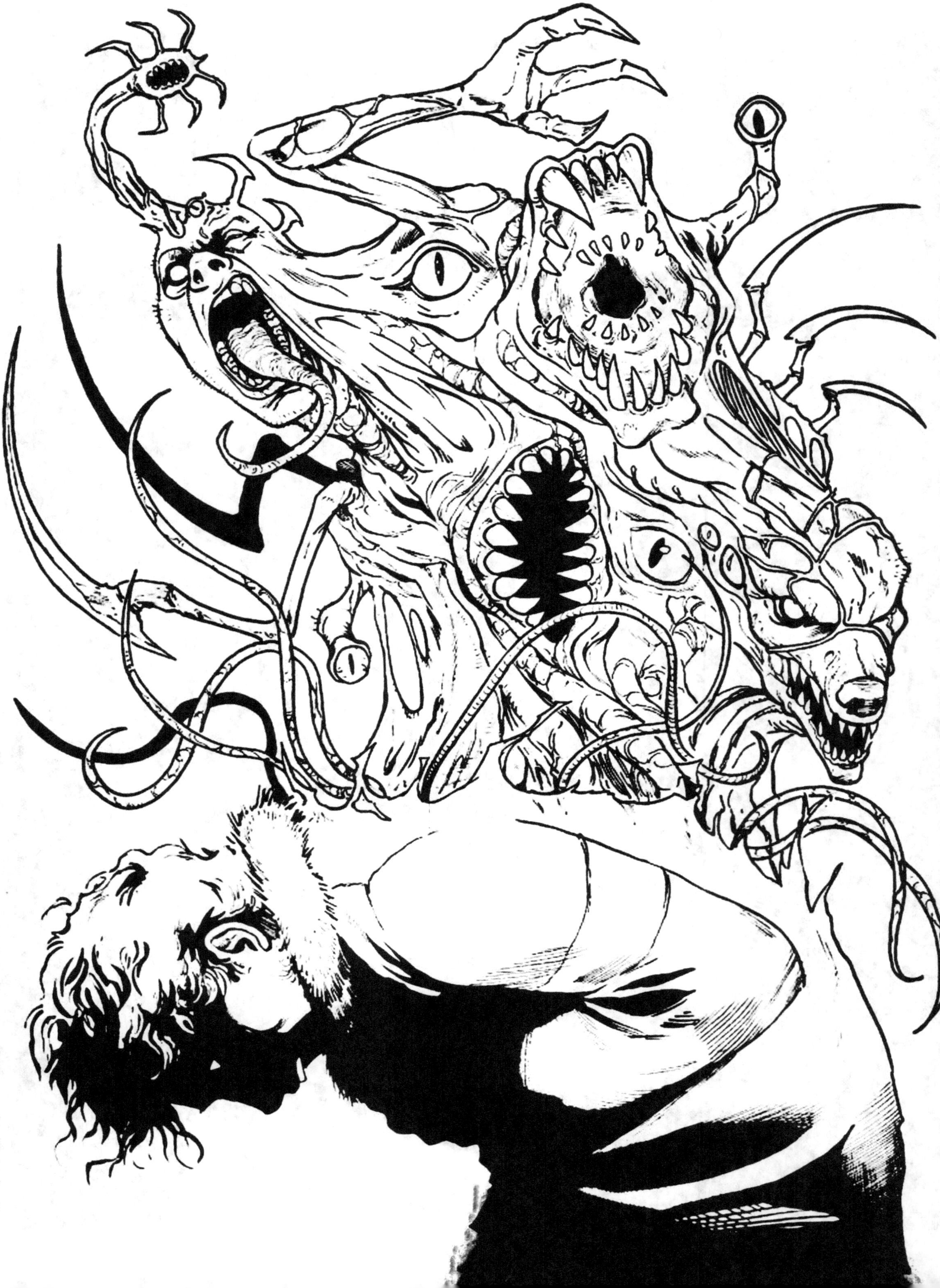

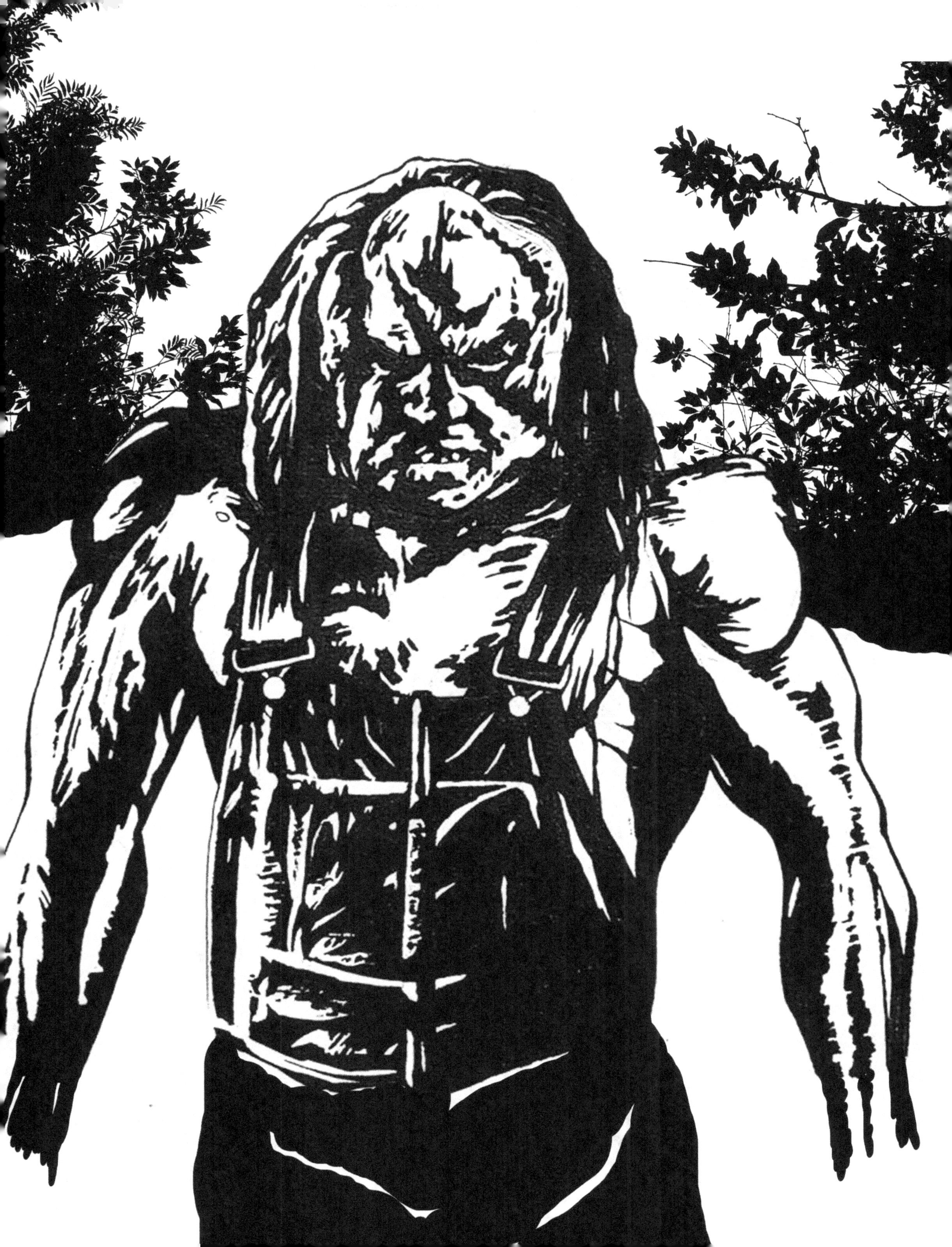

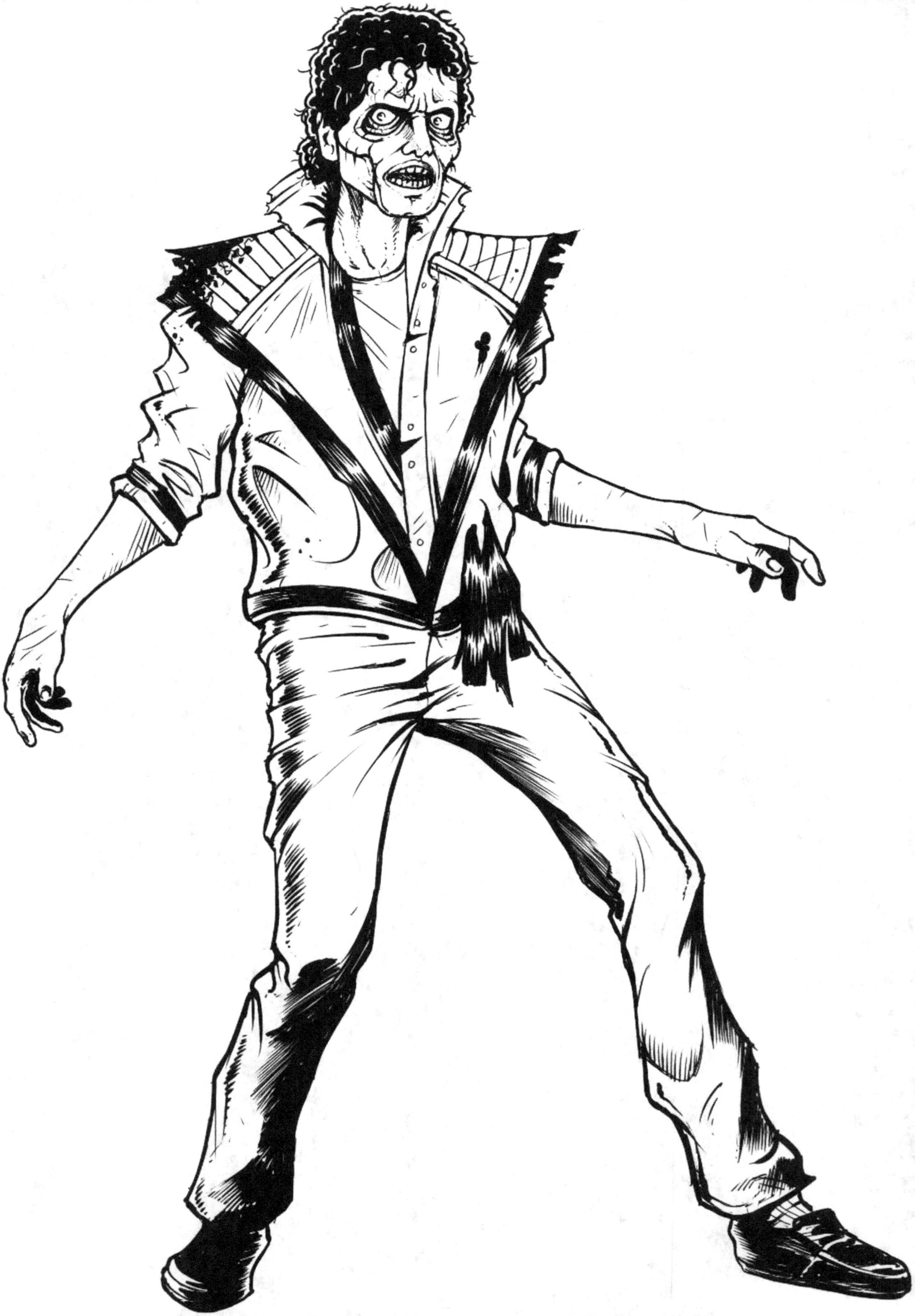

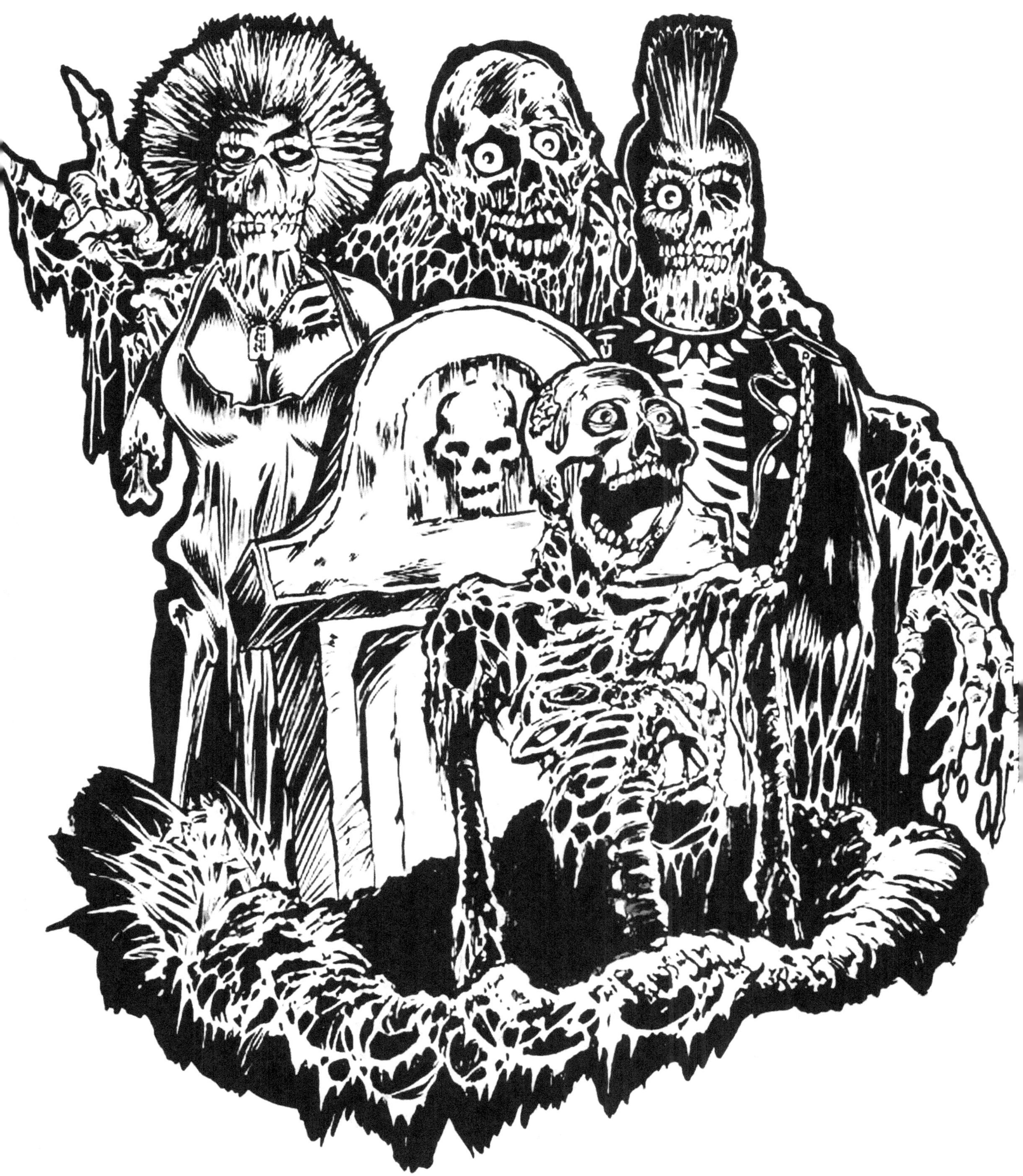

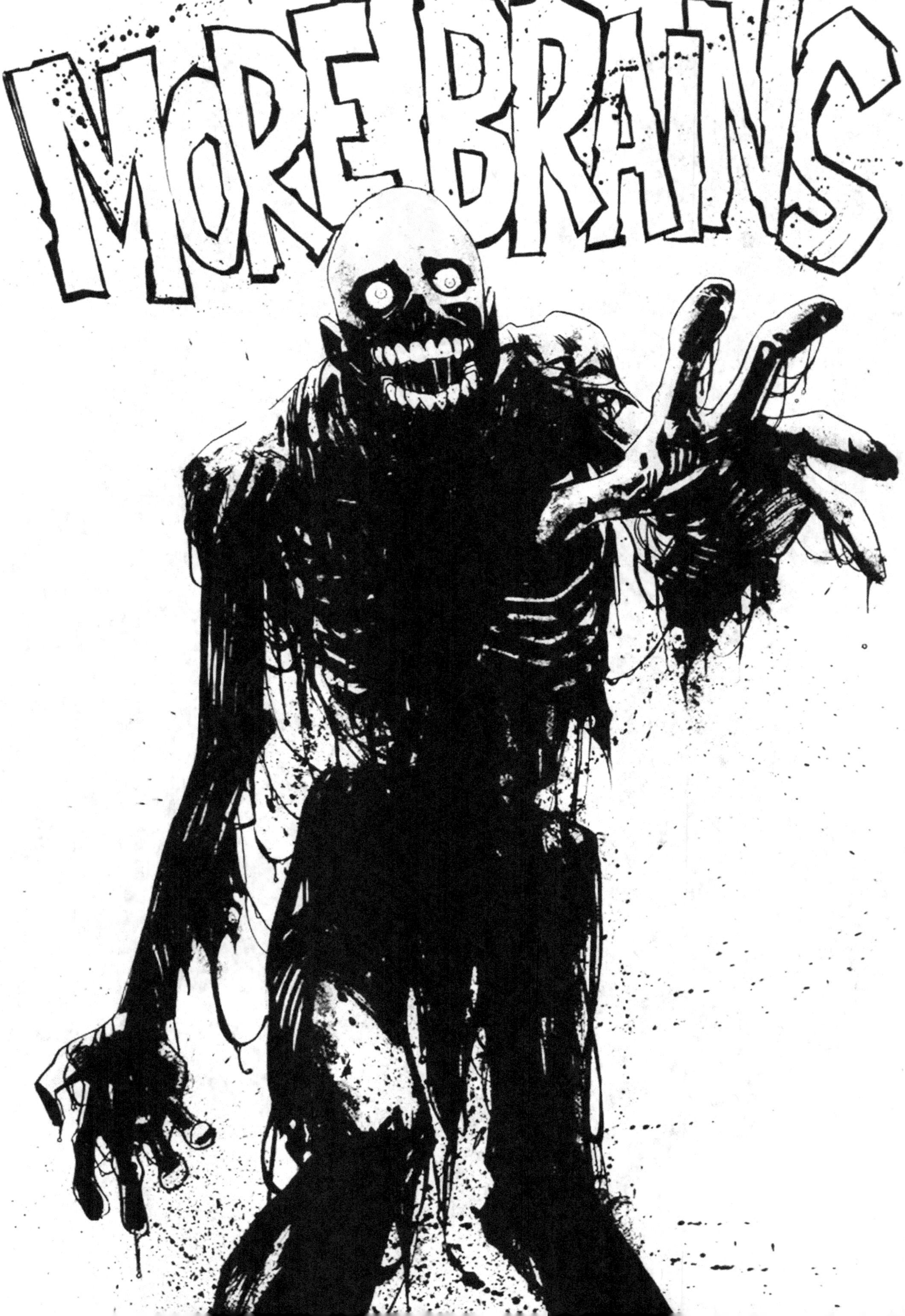
MORE BRAINS

www.ingramcontent.com/pod-product-compliance
Lightning Source LLC
Chambersburg PA
CBHW080138240526
45468CB00009BA/2527